ITTEN & DIRECTED
ROB ZOMBIE
OUSE
OF

HOUSE OF 1000 CORPSES

BY ROB ZOMBIE

HOUSE
OF
1000
CORPSES

BY ROB ZOMBIE

SAN RAFAEL • LOS ANGELES • LONDON

HOUSE OF 1000 CORPSES

This book is dedicated to the memory of

DENNIS FIMPLE
1940-2002

MATTHEW McGRORY
1973-2005

HARRISON YOUNG
1930-2005

KAREN BLACK
1939-2013

TOM TOWLES
1930-2015

IRWIN KEYES
1952-2015

MICHAEL J. POLLARD
1939-2019

SID HAIG
1939-2019

Welcome to the House of 1000 Corpses book. Contained within these pages is my original shooting script - complete with all my handwritten notes, scribbles, dialogue changes and other random bits and pieces of a constantly changing film. It was a long unconventional process to bring this monster to life and I wanted this book to reflect that insane journey.

From my early character sketches to finished blue prints of the murder ride you can follow the making of the film from start to finish. House of 1000 Corpses started out as a simple little horror film but somehow along the way it became much more... it became a labor of love for all involved.

After getting dumped by two different studios and sitting on a shelf for several years the film was finally released. Was it a smash? Nope, but it soon became something else... a true cult movie kept alive on word of mouth by an ever growing fanbase.

Now more than 20 years later it is more popular than ever... and for that I thank you.

— Rob Zombie

wolfensh

Ah, The Doctor is in. Don't Scream
Don't move... STAY Tuned for
Channel 68 Halloween Eve Movie
Marathon. I'm your host. The
Ghost Host with The Most.
Dr. Wolfenstein... and I
will be with you until The
end.

TERROR!
THRILLS!
Hartman

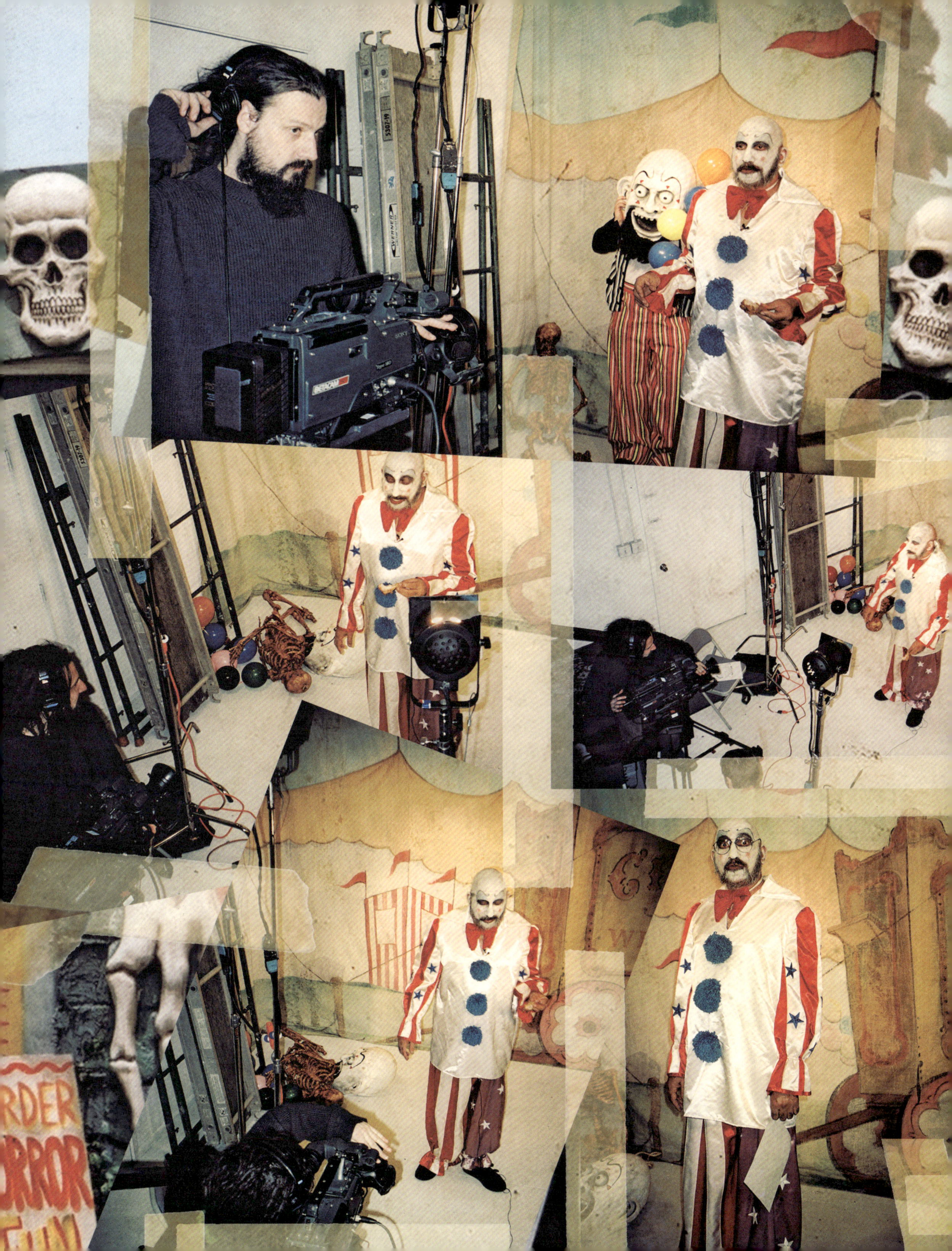
RDER
RROR

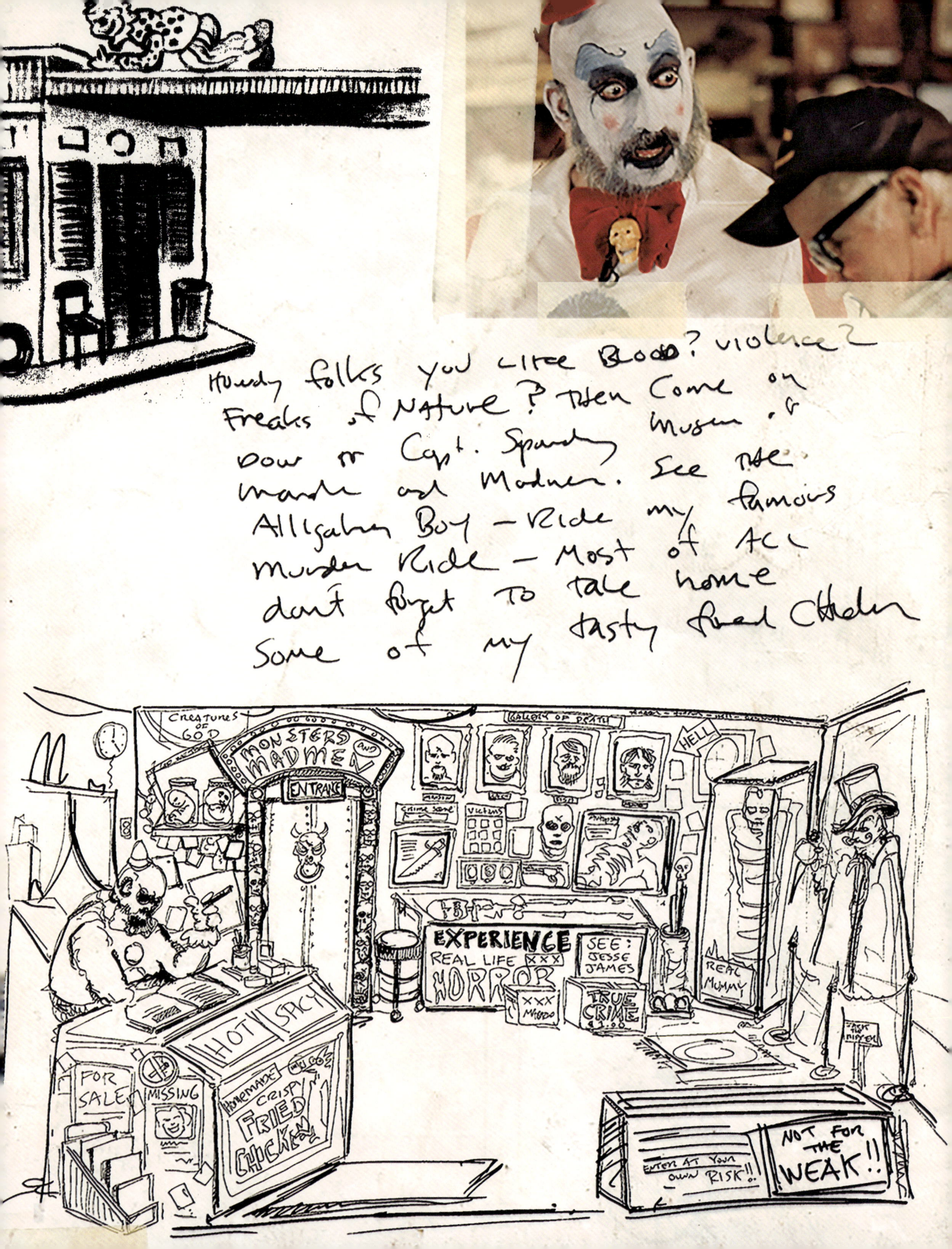
Howdy folks you like Blood? violence?
Freaks of Nature? Then come on
down to Capt. Spaulding Museum of
Murder and Madness. See the famous
Alligator Boy - Ride my
Murder Ride - Most of all
don't forget to take home
some of my tasty fried chicken
CREATURES OF GOD
MONSTERS AND MADMEN
ENTRANCE
GALLERY OF DEATH
HELL
Crime scene
Victims
EXPERIENCE
REAL LIFE XXX
HORROR
SEE: JESSE JAMES
XXX
TRUE CRIME
REAL MUMMY
HOT SPICY
HOMEMADE CRISP FRIED CHICKEN
FOR SALE
MISSING
ENTER AT YOUR OWN RISK!!
NOT FOR THE WEAK!!

CAPTAIN SPAULDINGS MUSEUM of MONSTERS AND MADMEN
TRUE HORROR
FRIED CHICKIN' AND GASOLINE
YOU WONT BELIEVE YOUR EYES
NO SISSYS
FUN 4 THE WHOLE FAMILY
STRANGE BUT TRUE
PHONE
TAKE THE TOUR $5
1000 CORPSES — SPAULDING'S MUSEUM
Captain Spaulding MUSEUM OF MONSTER & MADMEN
TAKE THE RIDE
FRIED CHICKEN
NOT FOR SISSIES
ENTER AT OWN RISK
SEE THE 2 HEADED BABY
SEE THE AMAZING 2 HEADED BABY
AMAZING RIDE
$5
1000 CORPSES — CAPT. SPAULDINGS MUSEUM OF MONSTERS + MADMEN

FADE IN :

1 INT. OLD HOUSE - LIVING ROOM - NIGHT 1

We see a LITTLE GIRL dancing around in a grainy super 8 home movie. A LITTLE BOY wearing a monster MASK enters the frame. He struggles to lift a double barrel shotgun. He points it at the girl and pretends to SHOOT.

GIRL
(voice over, whispering slowly)
Once I had a cat, he was the sweetest little guy. Then one day he got sick and died. My heart was broken. My whole body hurt.

She continues dancing. The little boy imitates her.

GIRL (CONT'D)
After that I saw things differently, everything could be summed up with three simple words... fuck the world.

The camera swings over to some ugly, toothless relations watching the show. They laugh.

2 EXT. SPAULDING'S - NIGHT 2

We open on a dark, lonely stretch of two lane blacktop. Off to the side of the road we see a rundown gas station.

RADIO ANNOUNCER
(V.O.)
Hey, welcome back to 93.5 WJRC's Halloween monster weekend. I'm Jimmy Ray and I'll be bringing you the oldies, goldies and sometimes the moldies. The good, the bad and the uglies straight from the WJRC vaults.

A weathered wooden sign proclaims CAPTAIN SPAULDING'S WORLD OF MONSTERS AND MADMEN, sits atop the building. A smaller sign below reads FRIED CHICKEN AND GASOLINE.

RADIO ANNOUNCER (CONT'D)
Hey, kids still trying to decided on just the right costume? We'll why not head on down to Randall's Penny Save located on Kimball Rd. just off route 1 in Mackin County. Choose from a wide array of ghost and ghouls, jeepers and creepers...
(scary sound effects)
...everything you need for your Halloween needs.

(CONTINUED)

MADMAN ARMED WITH BOMBS
Plastic Surgeon's Mistake Turns Man Into A Monster
BOY, 8, HACKS SISTER'S RAPE-KILLER TO DEATH
TOILET
FIND EVIDENCE IN MURDER PLOT
DEATH RIDES
BRUTAL FOOTPAD ABROAD
GREAT DETECTIVE SLAIN
MAIL BOX THIEF JAILED

WALL OF SHAME
THE BOSTON STRANGLER
ALBERT FISH
RICHARD SPECK
ED GEIN
KILLER FISH
OF GOD
AQUALINA
THE FEEGEE MERMAID
MUMIFIED PIG
WITH 7 FEET
AND 8 HOOVES

2 CONTINUED: 2

SHERIFF HUSTON, a tall southern good old boy, leans against his dusty cruiser smoking a cigarette, pumping gas into his tank.

3 INT. SPAULDING'S - NIGHT 3

Inside is a poorman's Ripley's Believe It or Not. Bizarre props and treasures of killers and monsters cover the dirty walls.

RADIO ANNOUNCER
(V.O.)
Alright let's get back to our monster music marathon with this classic called The Teddy Bear's Picnic.

Perched on a stool behind the counter sits SPAULDING, a crusty looking old man in a filthy clown suit and smeared make-up. The word LOVE is tattooed across his right knuckles and HATE is tattooed across the left.

He is reading a newspaper, crunching on crackers from a paper bag and halfheartedly listening to a small man wearing coke bottle glasses named STUCKY.

Stucky thumbs through a stack of autographed 8x10 photographs.

STUCKY
I..I got back a stack today. Some nice shots.
(holds up a picture of June Wilkinson)
See, a good topless June Wilkinson... unfortunately she personalized it...
(looking at the photo)
to Stucky love June.

SPAULDING
Hmmmmm.

STUCKY
Shit, this ain't worth nothing now that my name gotten all over it. I was a fix'in on trading it to Jackie Cobb.

SPAULDING
The retard over at Molly's fruit stand.

STUCKY
Yeah.

LOVE

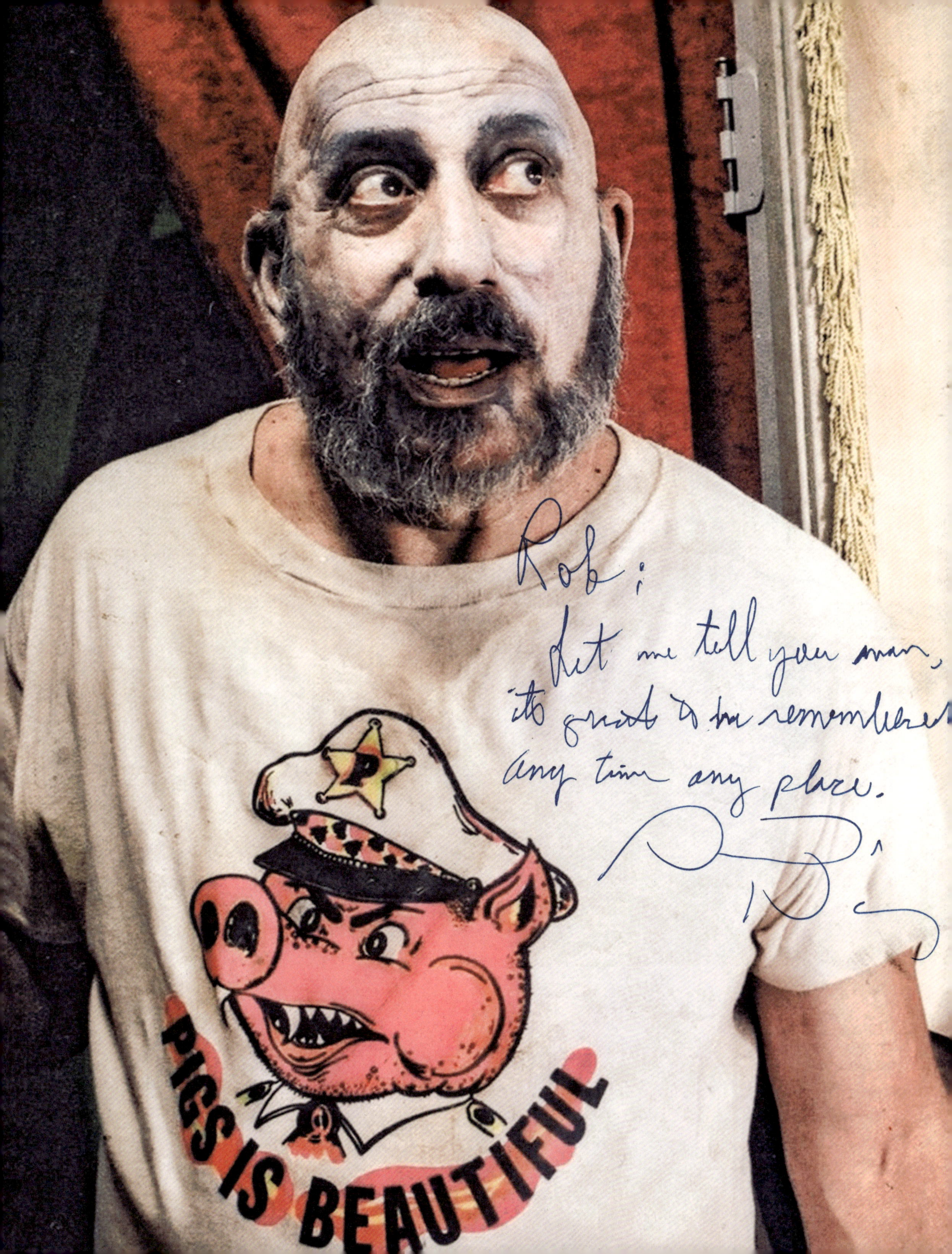
Rob;
Let me tell you man,
its great to be remembered
any time any place.
PIGS IS BEAUTIFUL

Spaulding brushes cracker crumbs off his paper and reading.

SPAULDING
Why you hang around that asshole I'll never know.

STUCKY
Yeah, that kid is one horny retard.

SPAULDING
Christ, ain't they all. All them retards wanna do is fuck and eat.

STUCKY
Well, yeah... I think that if you knew him... you might understand his urges,

SPAULDING
Worse than a fucking rabid baboon.

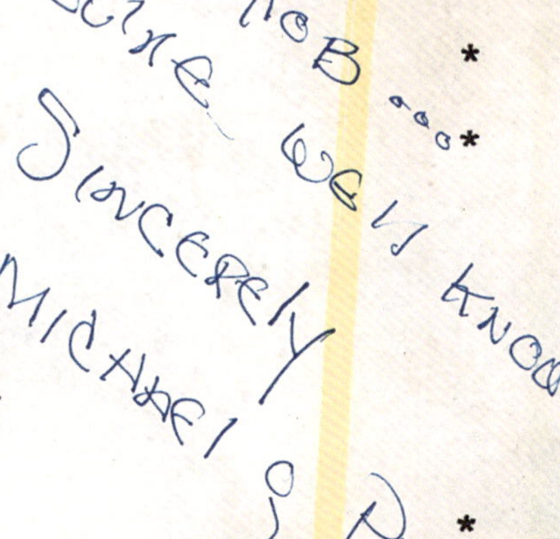

STUCKY
Yeah, I guess, You know next to wacking his weasel his other favorite thing is twisting sharpened pencils in the corner of his eyes.

Check artwork for Murder Ride.

SPAULDING
What?

STUCKY
Yeah, doesn't hurt himself, just spins it around next to his eyeball.

SPAULDING
I'm sure that ain't the only place he's sticking those pencils.

STUCKY
Naw, he don't do anything else with 'em, but he did get caught once with a Planet of the Apes doll hanging out his asshole.

SPAULDING
(laughing)
God damn.

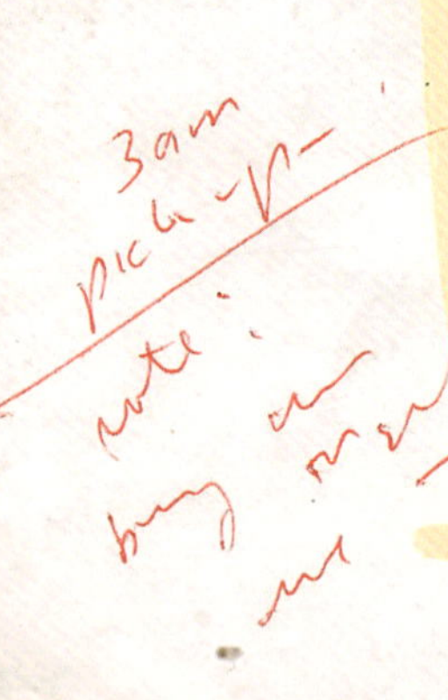

STUCKY
Had to take'em to the hospital. Kid had Dr. Zaius stuck half way up his butt, couldn't get it out.

HOUSE OF
1000 CORPSES

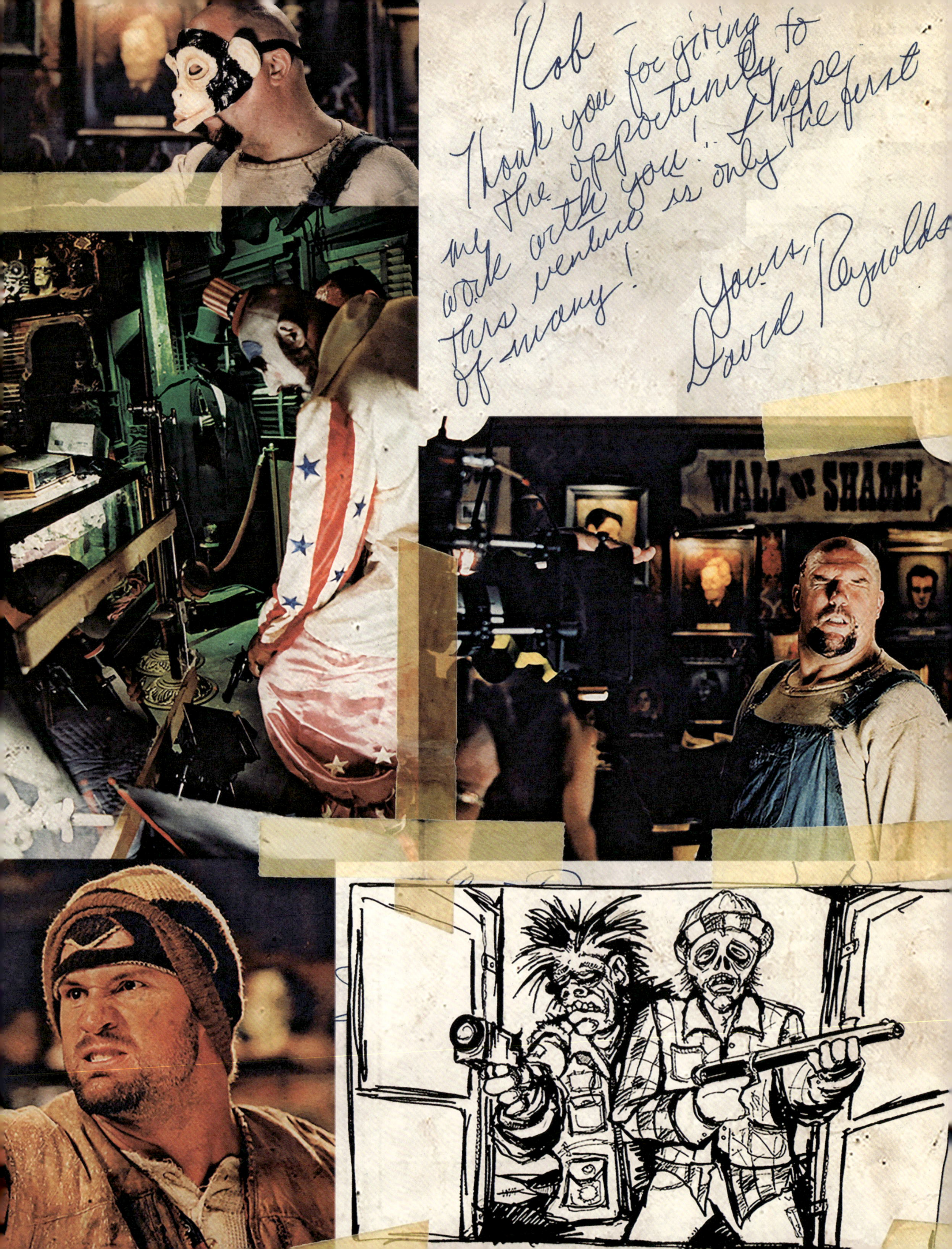
Rob –
Thank you for giving
me the opportunity to
work with you! I hope
this venture is only the first
of many!
Yours,
David Reynolds
WALL OF SHAME

3 CONTINUED: 3

SPAULDING
~~I always loved that mute broad that Chuck Heston was shacking up with.~~

STUCKY
~~Nova, yeah she looked pretty sweet.~~

SPAULDING
~~Yeah, now there's the perfect woman.~~

STUCKY
~~Can I get some stamps off ya?~~
~~(slapping down his money)~~
Did you fix the toilet yet?

~~Opens a drawer and tears off five stamps.~~

SPAULDING
Yes I did,.. so don't you go stuffin' any god damn paper towels down that hole. I just snaked the shit out of that thing.

Spaulding SLIDES the KEY attached to a cow skull across the counter. Stucky grabs it. Spaulding holds on.

SPAULDING (CONT'D)
Ya, hear me? You bust that crapper and I'll beat your ass.

STUCKY
I hear ya.

He lets go of the key.

4 EXT. SPAULDING'S - NIGHT 4

From a STRANGER'S POV we watch through the window, Stucky EXIT for the restroom.

KARL
~~You stupid dick, what were you thinking?~~

RICH
~~I'm sorry, it was the only one I could find.~~

KARL
~~I knew I should have left you home.~~

The Sheriff finishes pumping gas, gets in his cruiser and drives off.

DAVID REYNOLDS

SAG

HEIGHT: 6'4"
EYES: Hazel
HAIR: Black

Shirley Wilson & Assoc. Inc.
5410 Wilshire Blvd, Suite 806, Los Angeles, CA 90036
tel (323) 857-6977 • fax (323) 857-6980

Demo Reel Available Upon Request

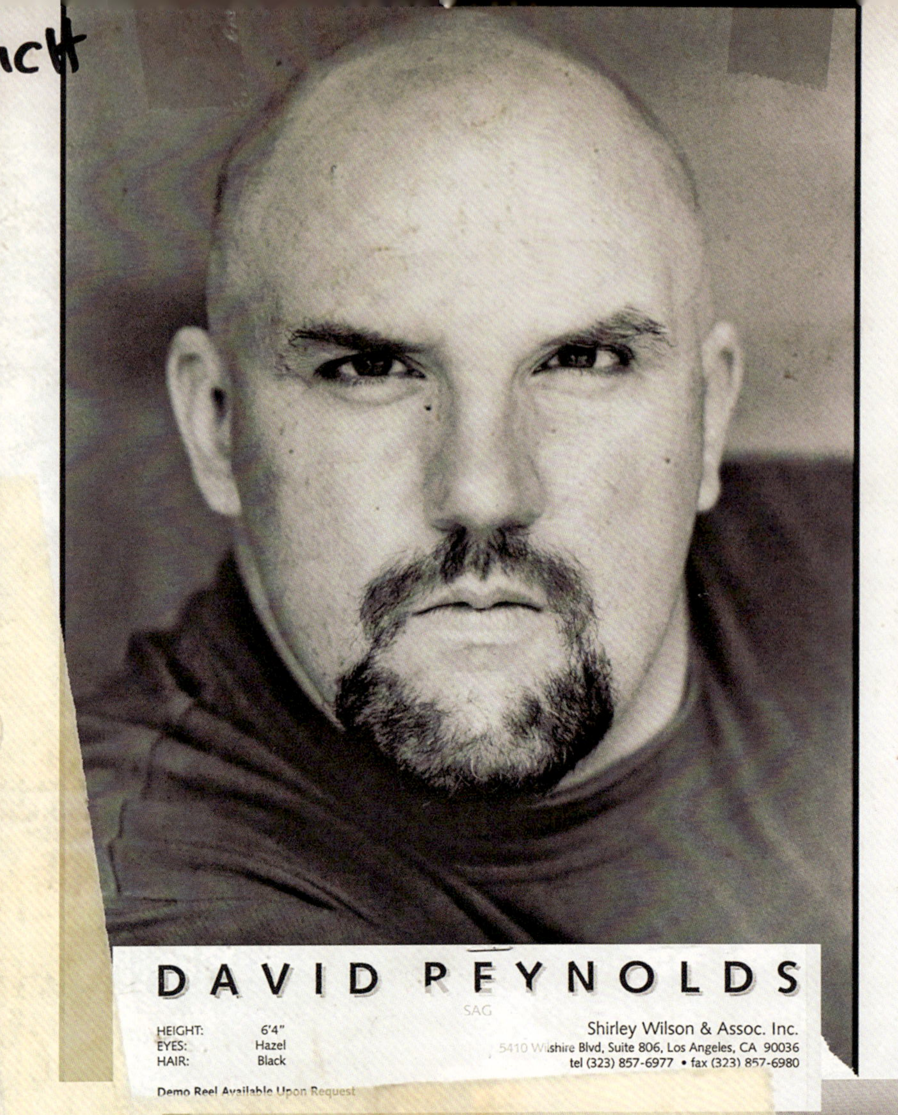

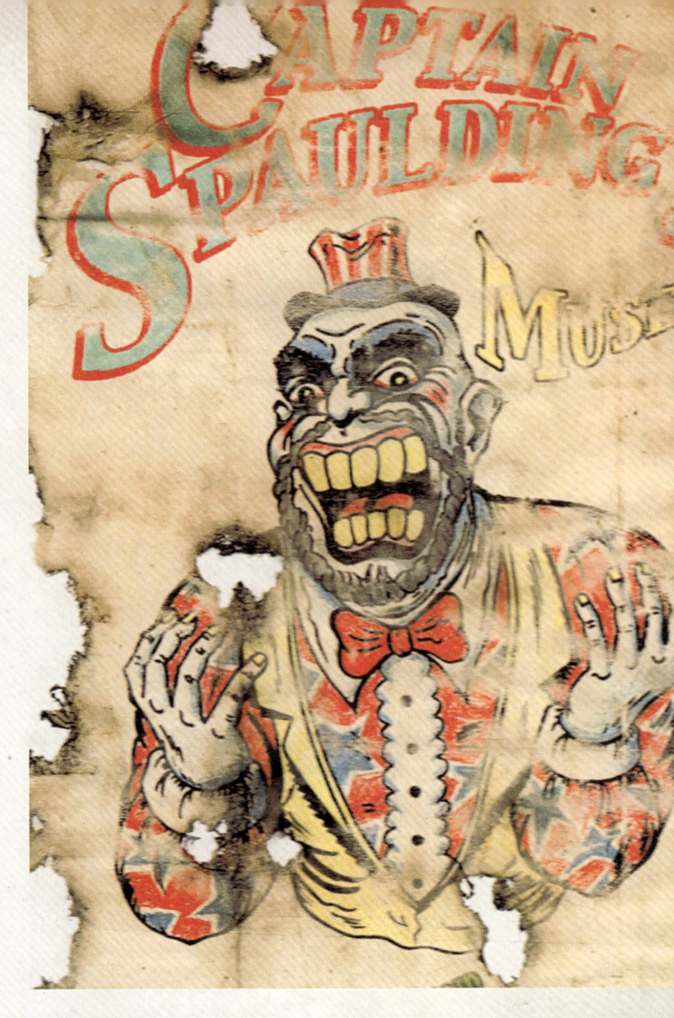

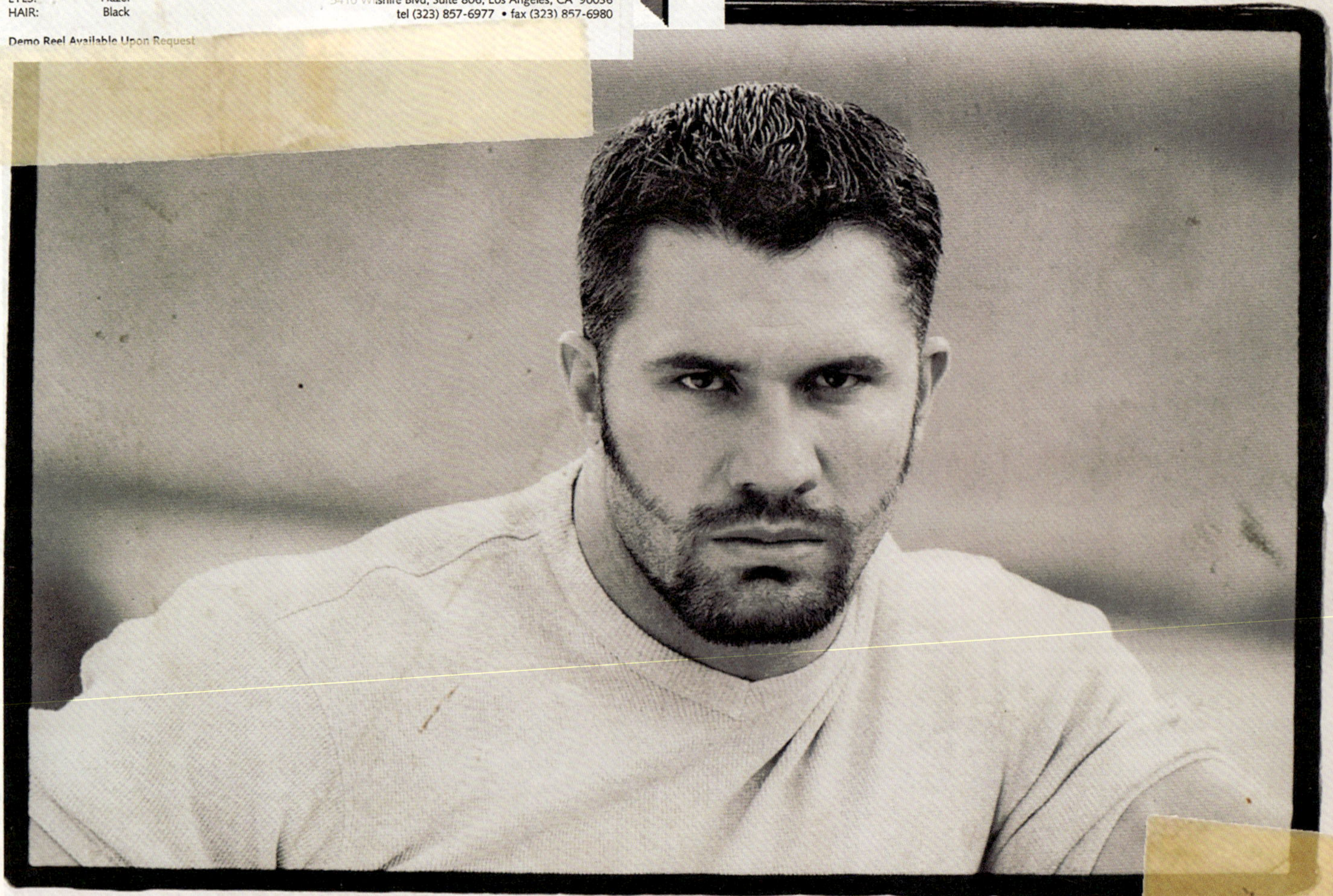

CHAD BANNON

Captain Spaulding
Zombie

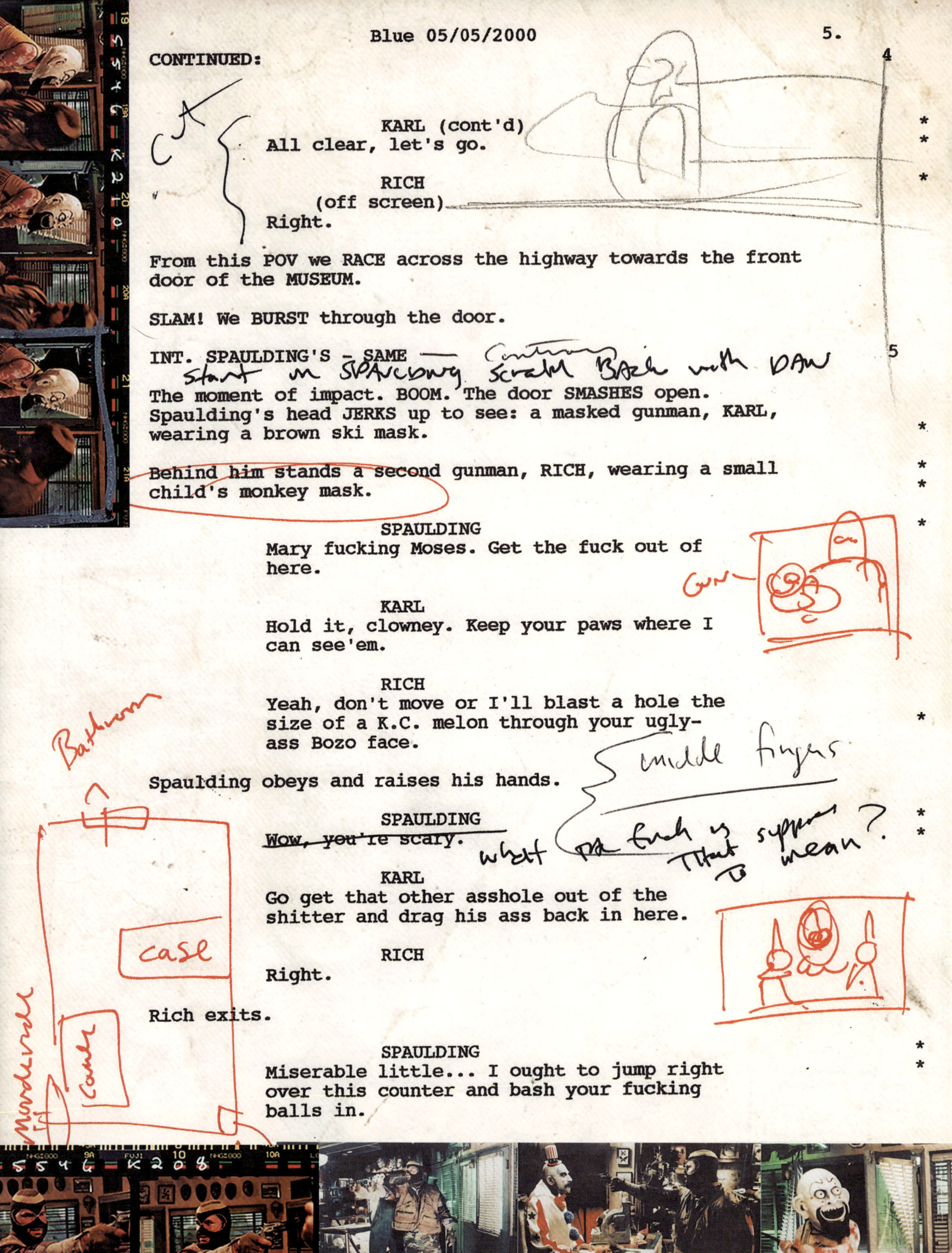

CONTINUED: 4

KARL (cont'd)
All clear, let's go. *

RICH
(off screen)
Right.

From this POV we RACE across the highway towards the front door of the MUSEUM.

SLAM! We BURST through the door.

INT. SPAULDING'S - SAME 5

The moment of impact. BOOM. The door SMASHES open. Spaulding's head JERKS up to see: a masked gunman, KARL, wearing a brown ski mask. *

Behind him stands a second gunman, RICH, wearing a small child's monkey mask. *

SPAULDING *
Mary fucking Moses. Get the fuck out of here.

KARL
Hold it, clowney. Keep your paws where I can see'em.

RICH
Yeah, don't move or I'll blast a hole the size of a K.C. melon through your ugly-ass Bozo face. *

Spaulding obeys and raises his hands.

SPAULDING *
~~Wow, you're scary.~~ *

KARL
Go get that other asshole out of the shitter and drag his ass back in here.

RICH
Right.

Rich exits.

SPAULDING *
Miserable little... I ought to jump right over this counter and bash your fucking balls in. *

House of 1000
Corpses

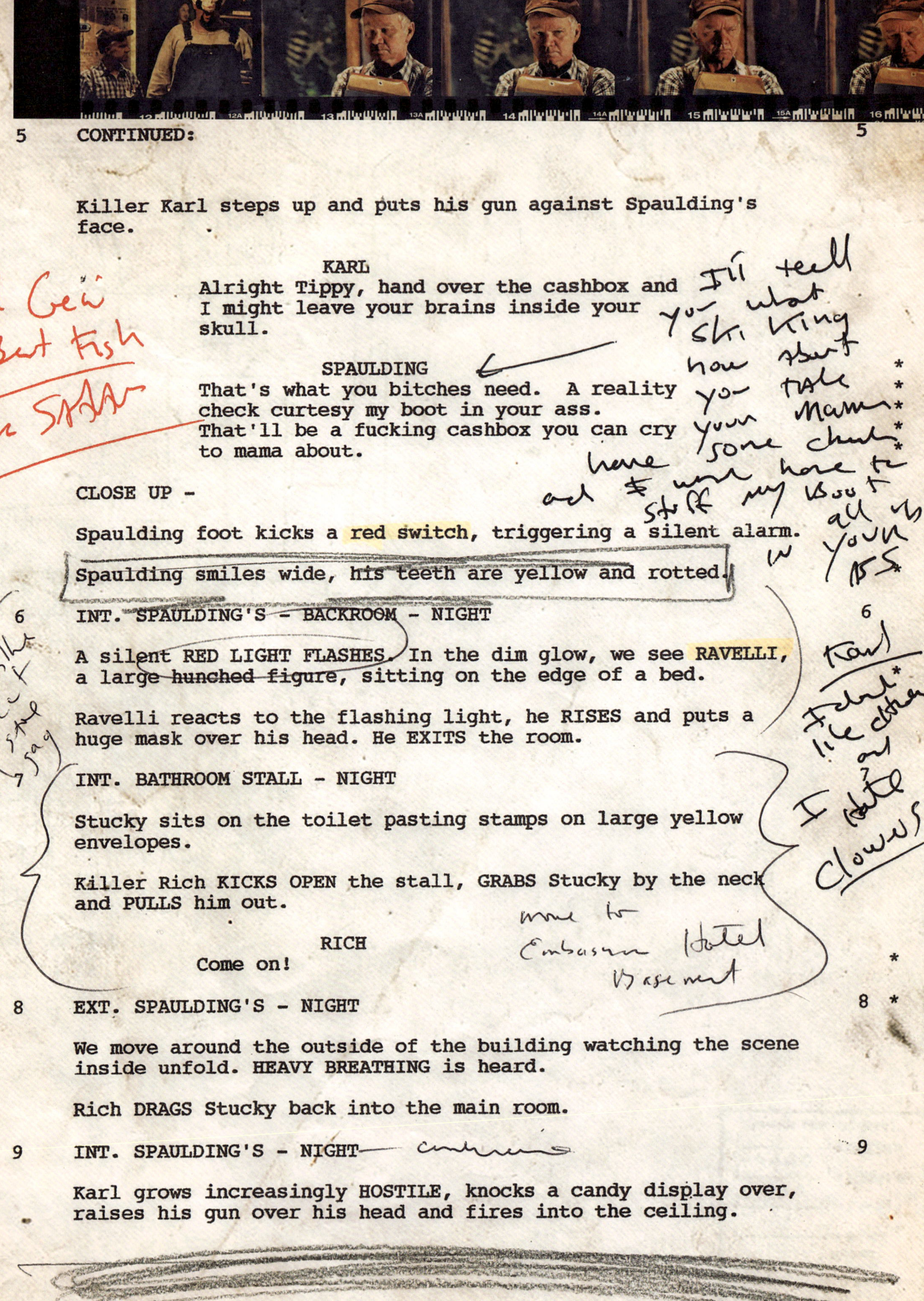

5 CONTINUED: 5

Killer Karl steps up and puts his gun against Spaulding's face.

KARL
Alright Tippy, hand over the cashbox and I might leave your brains inside your skull.

SPAULDING
That's what you bitches need. A reality check curtesy my boot in your ass. That'll be a fucking cashbox you can cry to mama about.

CLOSE UP -

Spaulding foot kicks a red switch, triggering a silent alarm.

Spaulding smiles wide, his teeth are yellow and rotted.

6 INT. SPAULDING'S - BACKROOM - NIGHT 6

A silent RED LIGHT FLASHES. In the dim glow, we see RAVELLI, a large hunched figure, sitting on the edge of a bed.

Ravelli reacts to the flashing light, he RISES and puts a huge mask over his head. He EXITS the room.

7 INT. BATHROOM STALL - NIGHT

Stucky sits on the toilet pasting stamps on large yellow envelopes.

Killer Rich KICKS OPEN the stall, GRABS Stucky by the neck and PULLS him out.

RICH
Come on!

8 EXT. SPAULDING'S - NIGHT 8

We move around the outside of the building watching the scene inside unfold. HEAVY BREATHING is heard.

Rich DRAGS Stucky back into the main room.

9 INT. SPAULDING'S - NIGHT 9

Karl grows increasingly HOSTILE, knocks a candy display over, raises his gun over his head and fires into the ceiling.

(CONTINUED)

IRWIN KEYES

9 CONTINUED: 9

KARL
(screaming)
That's it. I'm gonna count to ten and you're gonna hand over the cash or I'm gonna splatter your greasepaint mug across the stateline... one.

SPAULDING
Fuck your mother. *

KARL
Two.

SPAULDING
Fuck your sister. *

RICH
What are we gonna do? *

STUCKY
(recognizing Rich's voice)
Hey, I know you. You work at the hardware store, right?... Richard Wick...right? *

He looks nervously at Stucky.

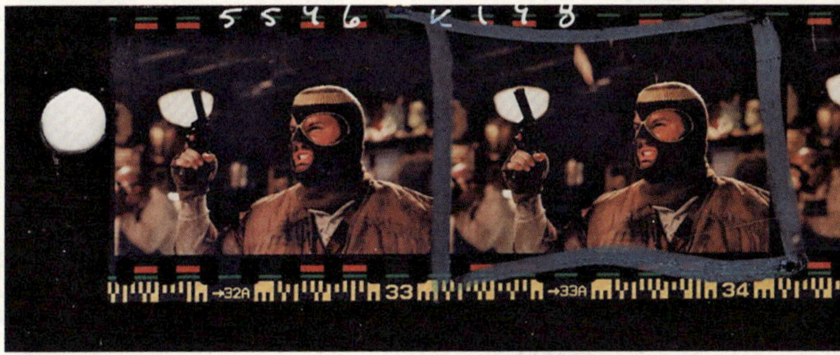

RICH
Shut your trap!

KARL
Quiet down... three.

SPAULDING
Fuck your grandmother.

STUCKY
Yeah, I remember now, all the guys at the store call you Little Dick Wick. Think the kids made up a song to go with that. *

RICH
(temper rising)
Shut up !

STUCKY
(singing)
Little dick wick, play with his prick
Don't his smell, just make you sick.

RICH
Stop singing...I hate that song!

take off mask — falls to the floor

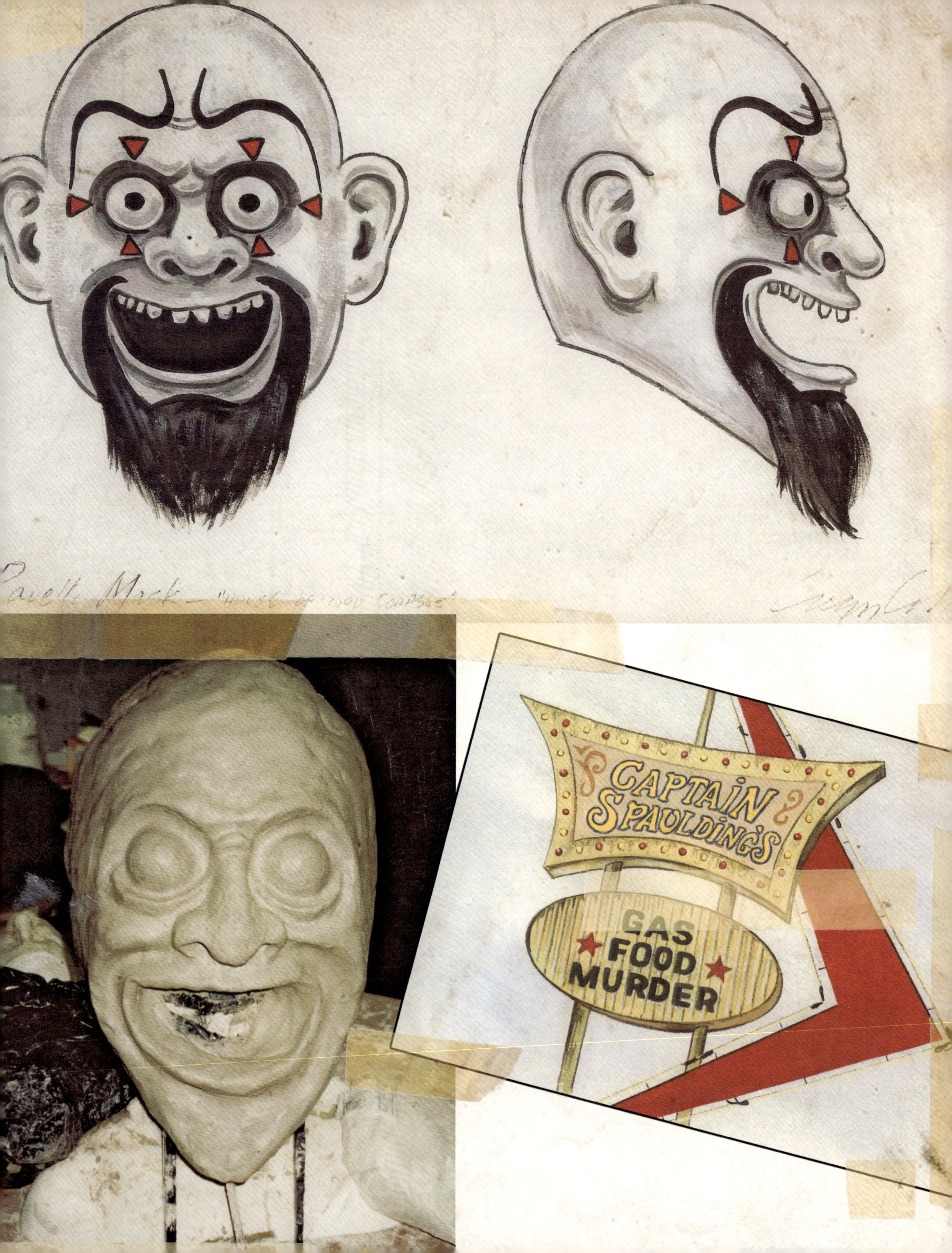
CAPTAIN SPAULDING'S
GAS
FOOD
MURDER

KODAK 400NC
21
KODAK 400NC
20
KODAK 400NC
19
KODAK 400NC
18
KODAK 400NC

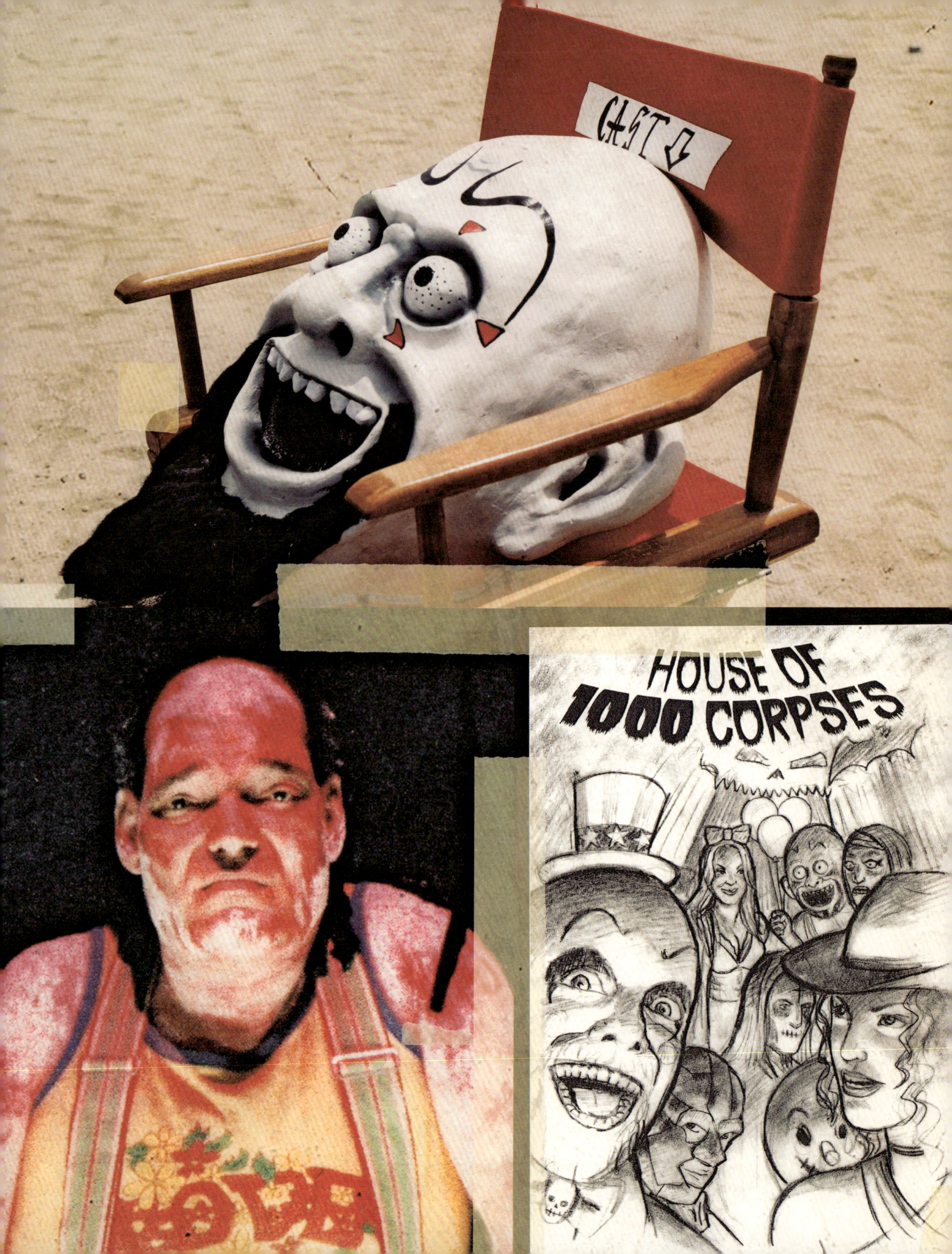
CAST
HOUSE OF
1000 CORPSES

10 EXT. SPAULDING'S - NIGHT 10 *

From Ravelli's POV watch through the window, as everybody inside starts SHOUTING at each other.

Suddenly, Rich SHOOTS Stucky. Stucky FALLS BACKWARDS against the wall, screaming in pain.

We move QUICKLY towards the entrance.

11 INT. SPAULDING'S - NIGHT 11 *

Suddenly... CRASH! Ravelli SMASHES through the front door knocking Karl to the ground. In the light we see that Ravelli is wearing an OVERSIZED CLOWN HEAD and large clown pants. In his hand is a sledgehammer. *

Rich TURNS towards the COMMOTION. The Captain quickly WHIPS OUT a GUN and FIRES. Rich falls dead.

Ravelli lunges at Karl, smashing him over the head with a the hammer. Ravelli's clown head comes loose and falls to the floor. We now see that Ravelli is a bald pitbull of a man with badly scarred skin that is painted white and red.

Karl hits the floor and begins CONVULSING violently.

Spaulding STEPS DOWN from behind the counter, puts his foot on Karl's throat and points his pistol at Karl's head.

SPAULDING *
And most of all... fuck you!

BOOM! Spaulding SHOOTS Karl in the head.

The screen EXPLODES RED, then TURNS BLACK.

SPAULDING (CONT'D) *
(V.O.)
God damn it, that motherfucker got blood all over my best clown suit.

12 EXT. FIELD - DAY 12 *

A lone FIGURE wrapped in a white bedsheet, wearing a cheap skull mask stands in a field. We move into his eyes, they are glazed. The title "House of 1000 Corpses" comes on screen. *

13 EXT. COUNTRY ROAD - NIGHT 13

We see a BILLBOARD painted on the side of an ABANDONED TRUCK. The sign reads GOD IS DEAD.

ZOMBIE
KODAK 400NC

13 CONTINUED: 13

We turn to face the road as a car drives by.

BILL
(yawning)
God damn, I am so sick of driving

JERRY
Alright then, out of all of Manson's
chicks who do think is the hottest.

INT. CAR - FRONTSEAT - NIGHT 14

Fast food wrappers and road maps clutter the car's dashboard, a swinging monkey head dangles from the rear-view mirror.

Behind the wheel, the driver, BILL HUDLEY, 29, downs the last sip of coffee before crumpling the paper cup and placing among the other trash before him.

BILL
Without a doubt Sandra Good, all the way.

JERRY
Really? Huh...interesting.

BILL
What? She seems like a nice girl, I mean
the X in the forehead is kind of a turn
off, but...

Beside him rides, JERRY GILMORE, 30, slumped down in his seat, reading a magazine with a flashlight, feet hanging out the window.

JERRY
I thought for sure you'd say Lynette
Fromme.

BILL
Sqeaky! No way, she ain't that hot.

JERRY
She's got that snooty vibe you
dig...every girl you date had that vibe.

BILL
Yeah but, she reminds me of this chick
that I remember from fourth grade...
called a...shit, what did we call her?
(thinks for second)
Oh yeah, Patty Pee-pee Pants... when ever
see got called on by Miss Chumski, this
(MORE)

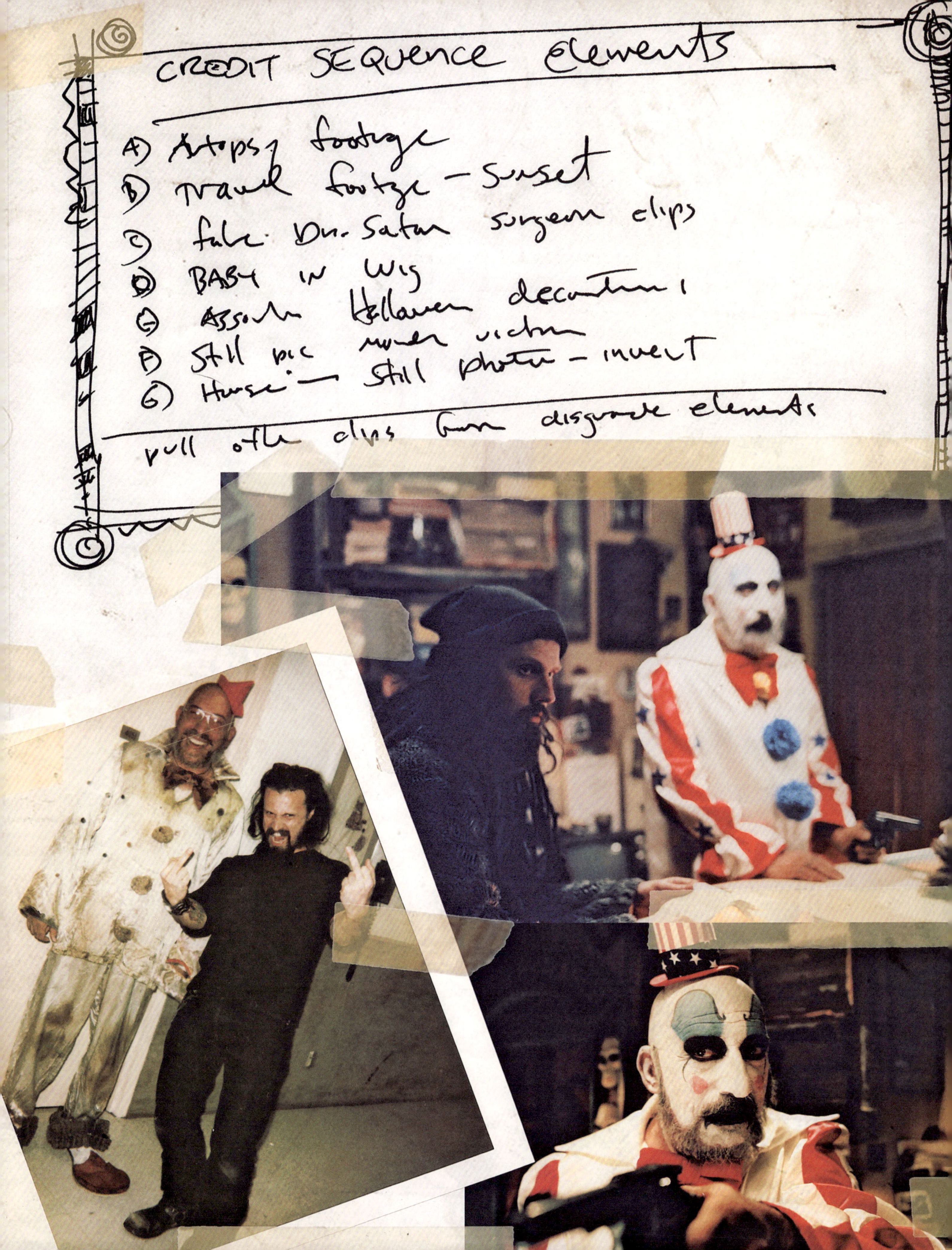
CREDIT SEQUENCE elements
A) Autopsy footage
B) Travel footage – sunset
C) fake Dr. Satan surgeon clips
D) BABY IN Wig
E) Assorted Halloween decorations
F) Still pic murder victim
G) Hearse – still photo – invert
pull other clips from disgrade elements

14 CONTINUED: 14

BILL (cont'd)
chick would piss in her pants and start balling.

JERRY
(laughing)
There always one kid with no bodily controls. We had this dude, Jeff Baxter, he was a puker. The fucker would just sit there puke all over himself.

BILL
Better that pissing... anyway so, what's your choice?

JERRY
If we're talking cute... like regular cute, I'd say Leslie Van Houton. *

BILL
Yeah, but we're not talking cute. *

JERRY
Alright, as far a hot goes I gotta go will... Ruth Ann Moorehouse. *

BILL
Oh yeah, I forgot about her. She was pretty hot.

JERRY
Fuck yeah, she is. I'd join a cult to get some of that stuff... and the best part *
is she didn't try to kill the President. *

BILL
Yeah, but she tried to murder a witness *
for the prosecution.

JERRY
I'll let it slide, she was only seventeen.

BILL
Yeah, I guess... hot chicks are always nuts.

JERRY
Hot has got nothing to do with it.

They high five. *

A14 EXT. COUNTRY ROAD - NIGHT A14

Off to the side of the road a billboard reads "If you lived here, you'd be home now." Bill's car drives passed. *

BILL
(yawning)
Hold on, I've heard this before... but I can't remember the end.

JERRY
So, the guy's goes to Hell and the devil says, "do you smoke?" The guy say," yeah"... the devil say, " great cause Tuesday is cigar night, sweetest Cuban cigars you ever had."

BILL
(surprised)
How is it possible that we are out of gas? What did you put in the tank? *

SAVE THIS BIT

JERRY
I dunno, two...three bucks. *

BILL
Three bucks! I told you to fill it. *

JERRY
Feel me, am I made of money? *

BILL
Jesus Christ, Jerry. *

JERRY
(not listening)
Then the Devil asks do you drink? Guy says, "yeah"... devil say," wonderful, Wednesday is free drinks night best booze you ever had... all made from the finest stuff."

BILL
Yeah.

JERRY
Then the devil says are you gay? Guy says," fuck no".. Devil says, " Well then, I guess you're gonna hate Thursdays."

BILL
Oh yeah, I remember now.

(CONTINUED)

WRITTEN & DIRECTED BY ROB ZOMBIE
HOUSE OF 1000 CORPSES
"A rock 'em, shock 'em horror carnival of screams!"
WWW.HOUSEOF1000CORPSES.COM
STARTS TODAY!
MANHATTAN
AMC
EMPIRE 25 42ND ST. & 8TH AVE.
11:50, 2, 4:15, 6:45, 9:20, 11:50
CITY CINEMAS
EAST 86TH STREET CINEMAS EAST 86TH ST. BETWEEN 2ND & 3RD AVES.
4:15, 6:15, 8:15, 10:30, 12:15AM
LOEWS 84TH STREET BROADWAY AT 84TH ST. 1-800-555-TELL
12:20, 2:40, 5:20, 7:50, 10:25, 12:35AM
LOEWS 34TH STREET 34TH ST. BET. 8TH & 9TH AVE. 1-800-555-TELL
11:30, 1:45, 4:15, 6:45, 9:15, 11:45
LOEWS 19TH STREET EAST 19TH ST. & BROADWAY 1-800-555-TELL
11:45, 2:15, 4:45, 7:15, 9:45, 12:10AM
LOEWS VILLAGE VII THIRD AVENUE AT ELEVENTH STREET 1-800-555-TELL
11:15, 1:45, 4:30, 7, 9:45, 12:15AM
UNITED ARTISTS THEATRES
BATTERY PARK STADIUM 16
12:10, 2:25, 4:40, 7, 9:15, 11:30
MAGIC JOHNSON THEATRES-HARLEM USA 125TH ST. & FREDERICK DOUGLASS BLVD 1-800-555-TELL
11:25, 1:45, 4:15, 6:45, 9:15, 11:45
BRONX
AMC
BAY PLAZA 13
NATIONAL AMUSEMENTS
CONCOURSE PLAZA MULTIPLEX CINEMAS
NATIONAL AMUSEMENTS
WHITESTONE MULTIPLEX
QUEENS
CINEPLEX ODEON
CINEMA CITY FIVEPLEX
CREATIVE ENTERTAINMENT
CINEMART CINEMAS
UNITED ARTISTS THEATRES
THE CROSSBAY 2
CREATIVE ENTERTAINMENT
JACKSON TRIPLEX
BROOKLYN
CREATIVE ENTERTAINMENT
CANARSIE TRIPLEX
UNITED ARTISTS THEATRES
COURT STREET STADIUM 12
CINEPLEX ODEON
FORTWAY CINEMAS 1-800-555-TELL
NATIONAL AMUSEMENTS
LINDEN BLVD MULTIPLEX CINEMAS
SHEEPSHEAD BAY
JAMAICA MULTIPLEX CINEMAS
KAUFMAN STUDIOS STADIUM 14
STATEN ISLAND
ALL STATEN ISLAND STADIUM 16 THEATRE
NO PASSES ACCEPTED
AND AT A THEATRE NEAR YOU!
I'M WITH STUPID

JERRY
Yeah, no shit I just told ya.
(looking at magazine)
Hey, you think this place called Alien Ed's UFO Welcoming center is still around?

BILL
I dunno.

JERRY
It says, "Where the Fact is separated from Fantasy."

BILL
Man, I really don't want to run out of gas out here in the middle of Pettycoat Junction, man.

JERRY
(sitting up)
Don't panic yourself, way too much caffeine guy.

BILL
Hey, I wouldn't need so much coffee if you'd ~~drive~~.

JERRY
You know I don't have night vision.

BILL
Yeah, I'm sure.

JERRY
Hey, pull over, I'll drive...I can't even make the lines on the road.

BILL
Forget it.

JERRY
There's a sign...
(reading the sign)
...Captain Spaulding's Museum of Monsters and Madmen...cool. Also...fried chicken and ...gasoline...next exit.

BILL
Fine...
(grumbling)
...guess your night vision kicked in.

(CONTINUED)

P.S. — Thanks for letting me be the good girl! and not typecasting ♥

Rob—

I can't even tell you how I feel about this movie... but I'll try. Your imagination, creativity, dedication and intelligence are inspirational. This has been an experience of a lifetime. Thanks to you, my kids will never be able to say that I was boring. Moreso, thank you for believing in me, and giving me this opportunity. You, and everyone you have surrounded us with on this film are quality people. "Good folk". You, Rob, are good people. I hope to make you proud.

All of my love,
Erin Daniels

ERIN DANIELS

JENNIFER JOSTYN

A14 CONTINUED: A14

The car drives pass. We turn and hold on the Billboard. We see the happy smiling face of a young Captain Spaulding.

15 EXT. SPAULDING'S - NIGHT 15 *

INSERT
Spaulding Attraction signs

The car pulls up to one of the gas pumps. Bill and Jerry get out. Inside we see Spaulding, now in army pants and a hunting jacket, mopping the floor.

BILL
I'll pump the gas. Go inside and see if it's worth thinking about.

JERRY
(salutes)
OK, ~~Boss.~~ Mr. Cranky,

Jerry walks inside and immediately comes back out.

JERRY (CONT'D)
Holy crap. You gotta see this place. It's boss. *

BILL
How boss? *

JERRY
Really fucking boss. *

BILL
Wake up the chicks and bust out the camera awesome?

Cut to
Bizarre skull man standing in middle of field - inversion

JERRY
Hell yeah.

BILL
Let's do it. *
*

16 INT. CAR - BACKSEAT - NIGHT 16

A dark haired girl, DENISE WILLIS, 27, sleeps curled up under a blanket, her face against the window. *

BOOM! Jerry pounds on the window. *

Hard cut

JERRY
(crazy voice) *
Wakey, wakey, eggs and bakey.. *

She opens her eyes.

(CONTINUED)

16 CONTINUED: 16

DENISE
Huh? What's wrong? *

JERRY
Come on, babe. Me and Bill found a kick *
ass place...grab Mary and come inside. *

Come on move, move!

Denise shakes a lump of jackets and sweaters lying next to her. She removes a sweater from the top of the pile to REVEAL the face of MARY KNOWLES, 29.

DENISE
Come on sleeping beauty, time to go to work.

need insert Bloody mop + Bucket

MARY
(half asleep)
Sleeping.

DENISE
Rise and shine.

MARY
(groggy)
No please, let me sit this one out.

DENISE
(removing the blanket)
Let's go. You're the one who wanted to be a photographer.

Spaulding needs clothes change

MARY
I resign.

Mary rolls back over.

DENISE
Too late. Your in for life, lets move it out Private Shutterbug.

MARY
(opening her eyes)
Christ, I hope this isn't more crappy folk art. It's so quaint... it's so primal... it's so crap.

DENISE
Aw, it ain't crap... it's ...cute
(sarcastic)
... and really who are we to judge the artistic merit of the tin-can Mona Lisa

HOUSE OF
1000 CORPSES

18 CONTINUED: 18

SPAULDING
Shit, I don't remember exactly. I took over for my Pa just after the Duke nabbed the Oscar.

BILL
The Duke?

SPAULDING
Yeah, my Pa wasn't right in the head after that.

BILL
You mean John Wayne?

SPAULDING
Hell, boy there some other Duke's you know about?
(rolls up his sleeve to reveal a John Wayne tattoo)
A greatest American who ever lived.

how many

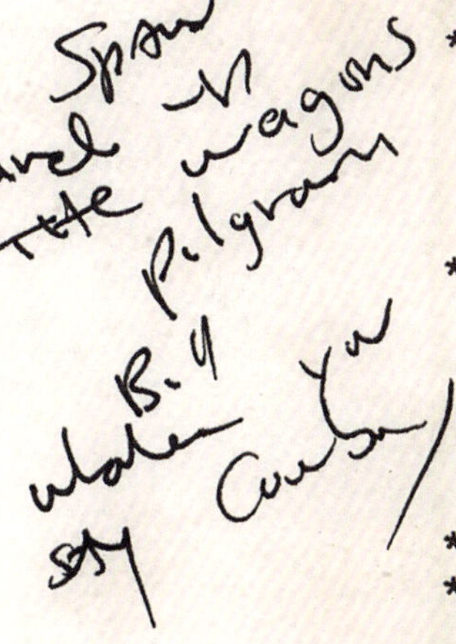

BILL
Yeah, I was never that big of a western fan. I like science fiction.

SPAULDING
A spaceboy, eh...I figured as much.

BILL
Well? (does robot sounds)

let me ask you something.

SPAULDING
Why the fuck you asking so many jackass questions for?

BILL
You see me and my friends are have been travelling cross-counrty, writing a book on offbeat roadside attractions. You know all the crazy shit you see when you drive cross country.

SPAULDING
I don't drive 'cross country.

BILL
But if you did.

SPAULDING
I don't.

"THE DUKE"

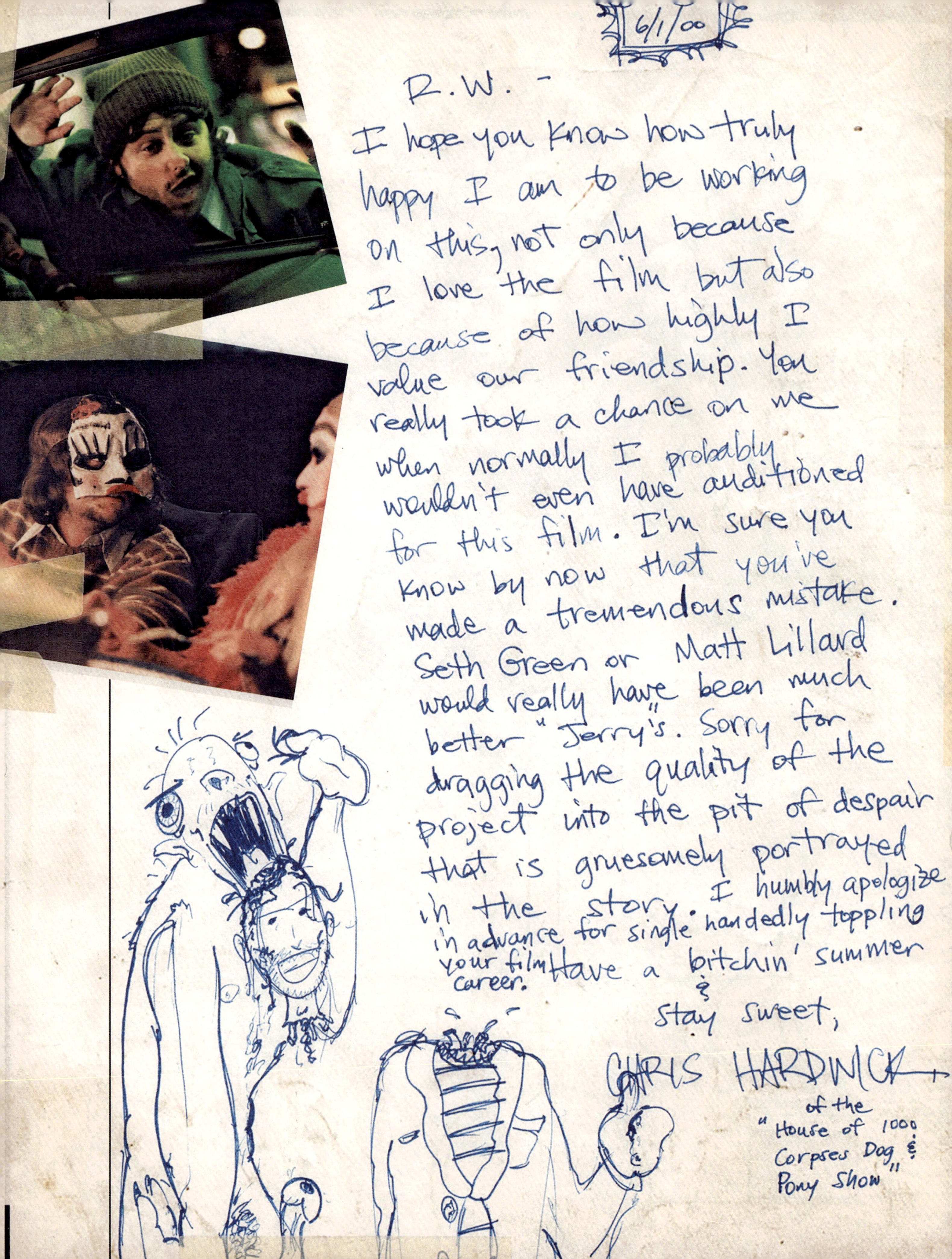

6/1/00

R.W. -

I hope you know how truly happy I am to be working on this, not only because I love the film but also because of how highly I value our friendship. You really took a chance on me when normally I probably wouldn't even have auditioned for this film. I'm sure you know by now that you've made a tremendous mistake. Seth Green or Matt Lillard would really have been much better "Jerry"s. Sorry for dragging the quality of the project into the pit of despair that is gruesomely portrayed in the story. I humbly apologize in advance for single handedly toppling your film career. Have a bitchin' summer & stay sweet,

CHRIS HARDWICK

of the "House of 1000 Corpses Dog & Pony Show"

18 CONTINUED: 18

BILL
But suppose for a second you did.

SPAULDING *
(fake hick accent)
Y'all find us country people real funny like don't ya... well, God damn pack up the mule and sling me some grits, I'ze a gotta get me some schooling.

BILL
No, no I think it's really interesting... *
I wasn't making fun of it. *

SPAULDING *
Well fuck me Side Sally, who want to read about all that horse shit anyway.

Jerry OVERHEARS Bill's and Spaulding's conversation and joins in to help.

JERRY
You'd be surprised. Would it be OK if we
included it in our book? You got some *
really rare stuff here... *
(pointing to Aqualina) *
... it dig your Feegee mermaid. *

SPAULDING *
Hey, knock yourself silly. *

19 INT. SPAULDING'S - RESTROOM - NIGHT 19

The restroom is gray, dingy, a single exposed light bulb hangs from the ceiling. The peeling walls are plastered with newspaper clipping and faded photos.

Mary is in the stall, sitting on the toilet, staring straight ahead at a poster. *

Denise stands at a tiny sink, splashes water on her face. She looks at herself in the mirror. *

DENISE
(water running down her face)
I swear I've aged five years since this trip started.

MARY
Tell me about it.

KEEP OFF! THE GRASS
I'M

19 CONTINUED: 19

DENISE
(takes a paper towel and wipes her face)
God, I hate falling asleep in the afternoon. Now I'll be up all night...
(stretches)
... ugh, my back is killing me.

MARY
Yeah, hey how far you think we are from your Dad's.

Mary flushes the toilet and exits the stall.

DENISE
I don't know. Couple hours I think. I've got to call him.

Mary washes her hands. Denise ties up her hair.

MARY
It will feel so good to have a few days off to regenerate. This trip is fun, but it's starting to get brutal.

DENISE
Yeah, I hit burn out mode back at Miss Bunny's place.

MARY
I know, That was some creepy shit.

DENISE
Watching her dance around with those ratty-looking animals was ridiculous.

MARY
Yeah, and disgusting...if I hadn't unfortunately seen it with my own eyes, I would never have believed it.

DENISE
A decent meal every once in awhile wouldn't hurt either, this road food is really doing a number on my insides.

MARY
If I never eat at another Waffle House again, I can die a happy girl.

DENISE
Scattered , smothered and covered.

8 8A 9 9A 10 10A 11 11A
14 GOLD 200-6 15 200-6 KODAK 16 GOLD 200-6 17 200-6 KODAK

19 CONTINUED: 19

MARY
Exactly... well, I guess a couple more photos won't kill me.

20 INT. SPAULDING'S - MAIN ROOM - NIGHT 20

Jerry is scanning every inch of Spaulding's, making notes. *

Bill leans against the wall next to him, sipping at hot cup of coffee.

The girls return from the bathroom. Jerry jumps up with excitement.

JERRY
Great, you're back. Let's go. We already paid for the tickets.

DENISE
Tickets for what?

JERRY
This isn't everything. Get ready for this.. there's a Museum of Murder and Mayhem.

DENISE
Aw Jerry, I don't want to see that. *

MARY
How about if we skip it and just hang out here. I can get some great shots of this stuff.

Jerry PULLS Denise over and puts his arm around her.

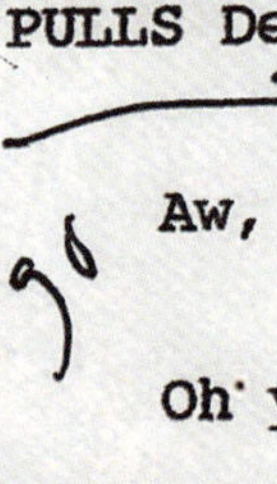

JERRY
Aw, come on. It will be fun.

DENISE
Oh yeah, murder museum... sounds fun.

Bill grabs Mary by the hand and kisses it.

BILL
(smiling)
We'll need pictures of the inside too.

MARY
Alright, alright. I know... I don't even wat to hear it. * *

Bill and Mary kiss.

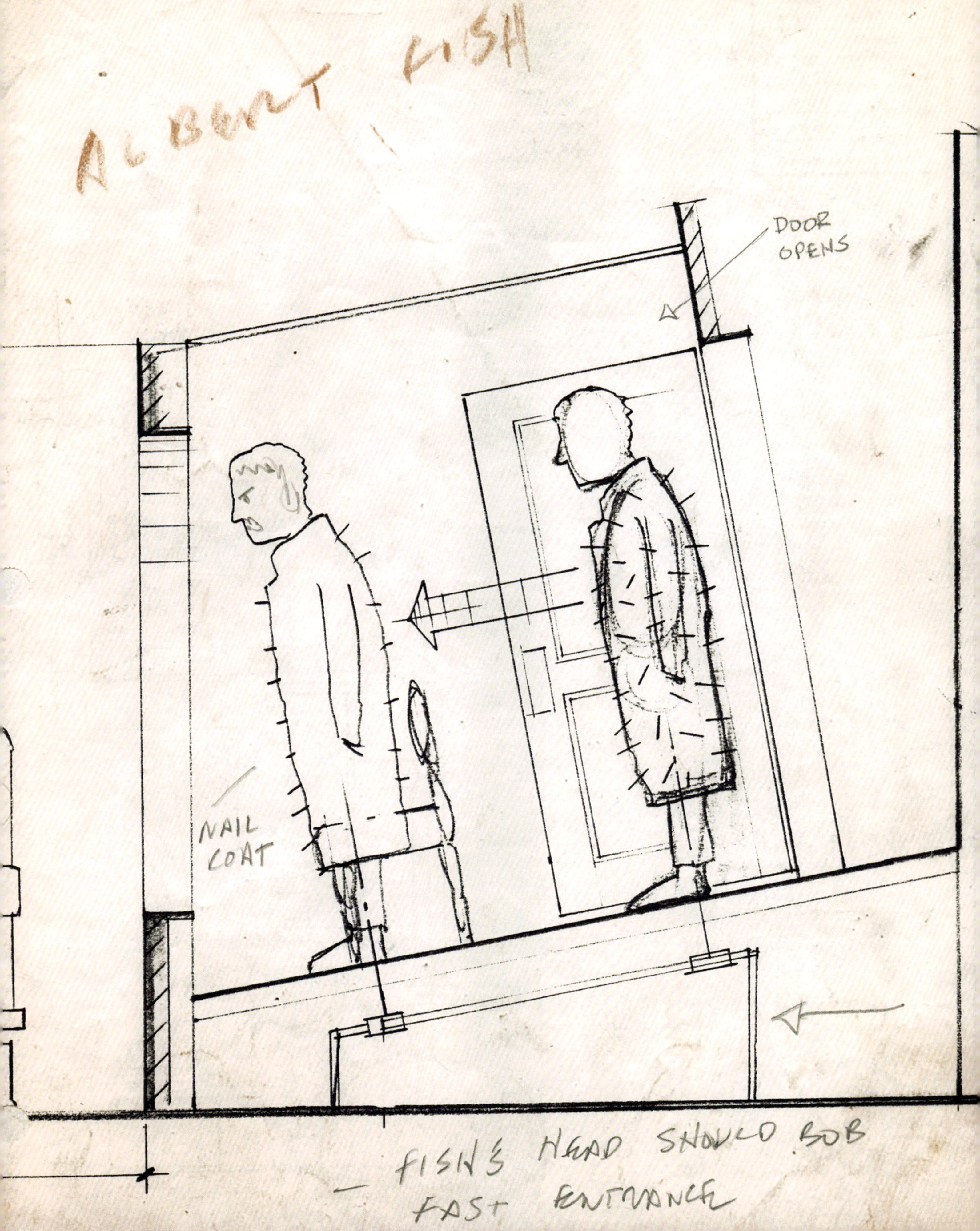

ALBERT FISH

DOOR OPENS

NAIL COAT

— FISH'S HEAD SHOULD BOB
FAST ENTRANCE

NOTE LOTS OF BLOOD

SECTION THRO

ENTRANCE
nter At Your Own Risk

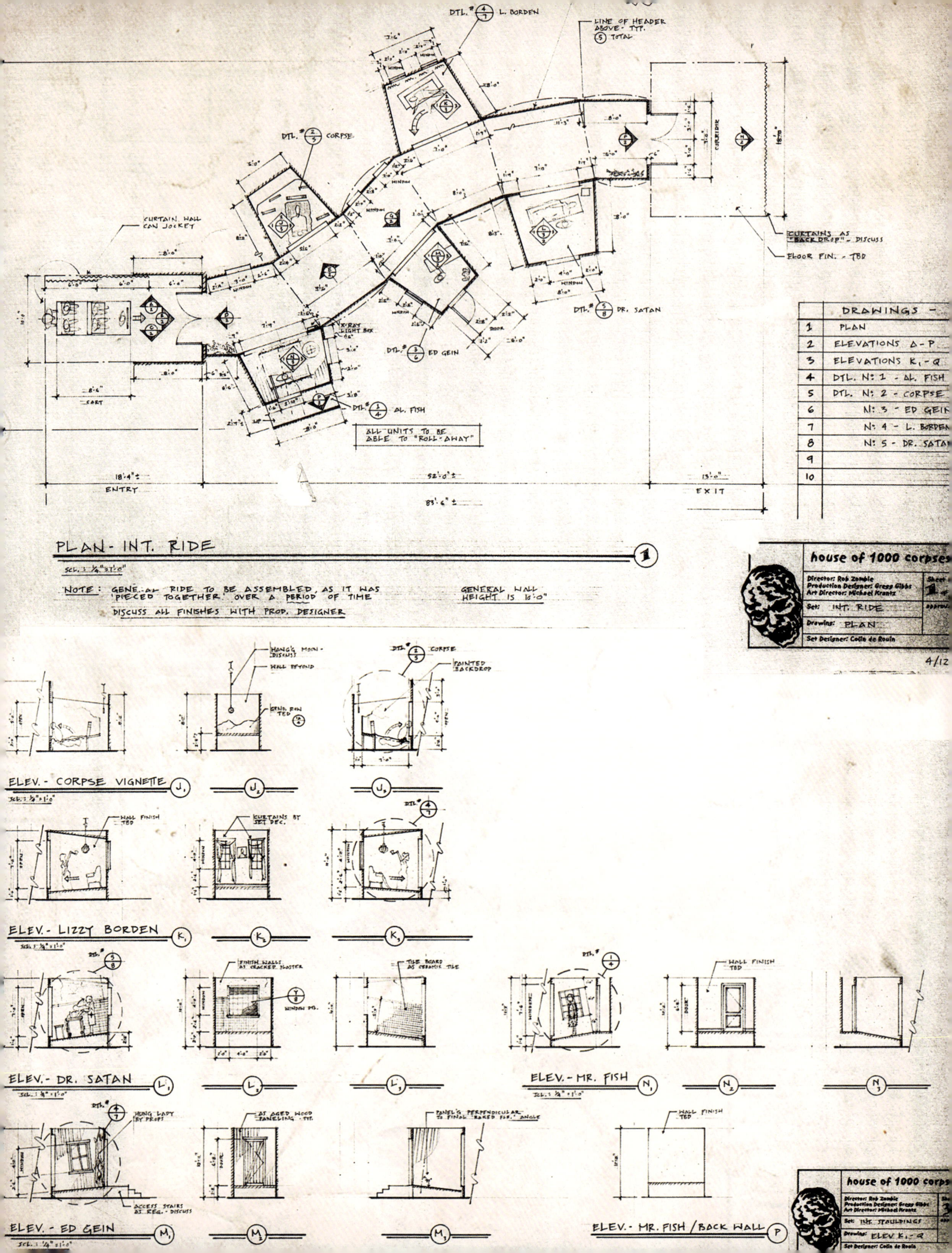

PLAN- INT. RIDE
SCL. : 1/4"=1'-0"
NOTE : GENERAL RIDE TO BE ASSEMBLED, AS IT WAS 'PIECED TOGETHER' OVER A PERIOD OF TIME
DISCUSS ALL FINISHES WITH PROD. DESIGNER
GENERAL WALL HEIGHT IS 16'-0"
ALL UNITS TO BE ABLE TO "ROLL-AWAY"
CURTAIN WALL CAN JOCKEY
LINE OF HEADER ABOVE - TYP. 5 TOTAL
CURTAINS AS "BACKDROP" - DISCUSS
FLOOR FIN. - TBD
DTL. # 4/7 L. BORDEN
DTL. # 2/5 CORPSE
DTL. # 5/8 DR. SATAN
DTL. # 3/6 ED GEIN
DTL. # 1/4 AL. FISH
X-RAY LIGHT BOX
CORRIDOR
CART
ENTRY
EXIT
18'-4" ±
52'-0" ±
13'-0"
83'-6" ±
DRAWINGS
1 PLAN
2 ELEVATIONS A-P
3 ELEVATIONS K1-Q
4 DTL. N: 1 - AL. FISH
5 DTL. N: 2 - CORPSE
6 N: 3 - ED GEIN
7 N: 4 - L. BORDEN
8 N: 5 - DR. SATAN
9
10
house of 1000 corpses
Director: Rob Zombie
Production Designer: Gregg Gibbs
Art Director: Michael Krantz
Set: INT. RIDE
Drawing: PLAN
Set Designer: Colin de Rouin
4/12
ELEV. - CORPSE VIGNETTE
J1 J2 J3
HANG'G MOON - DISCUSS
WALL BEYOND
PAINTED BACKDROP
ELEV. - LIZZY BORDEN
K1 K2 K3
WALL FINISH TBD
CURTAINS BY SET DEC.
ELEV. - DR. SATAN
L1 L2 L3
FINISH WALLS AS CRACKED PLASTER
TILE BOARD AS CERAMIC TILE
ELEV. - MR. FISH
N1 N2 N3
WALL FINISH TBD
ELEV. - ED GEIN
M1 M2 M3
HUNG LADY BY PROPS
AS AGED WOOD PANELING - TYP.
PANELS PERPENDICULAR TO FINAL "RAKED FLR." ANGLE
ACCESS STAIRS AS REQ. - DISCUSS
ELEV. - MR. FISH / BACK WALL
P
house of 1000 corpses
Director: Rob Zombie
Set: INT. STOULDINGS
Drawing: ELEV K1 - Q

20 CONTINUED: 20

Spaulding waits, unamused. He rolls his eyes.

SPAULDING
Anytime this year, people. Alright line your asses up in front of the black door. The tour is about to begin.

Spaulding steps down from behind the counter.

Spaulding and the kids enter a darkened room through strange painted metal.

21 INT. SPAULDING'S - MUSEUM - NIGHT 21

Darkness. A blue light comes on. Spaulding is standing on a MOTORIZED PLATFORM. Bill, Jerry, Mary and Denise are seated on the platform.

Ravelli stands behind ready to push the platform forward.

SPAULDING
Ravelli, let's go.

The tour begins.

4 seats

SPAULDING (CONT'D)
(speaking through a small megaphone)
Ladies and Gentlemen, you are about to enter a world of darkness. A world where life and death are meaningless and pain is God.
(Pointing with a cane)
To your left you see the infamous Albert Fish.

Spaulding into strange Uncle Sam outfit

A lifeless wax figure POPS forward with a loud metal CLANG. Mary jumps back with fright, after regainging her sense starts snapping pictures.

AL FISH - MORE BEA

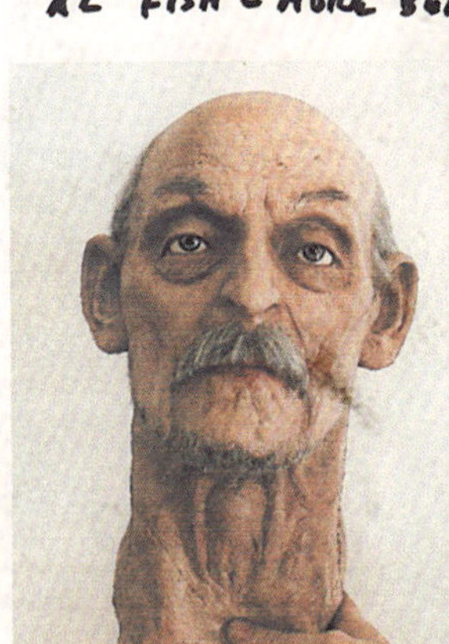

More Beard stubble

SPAULDING (CONT'D)
Sadist, masochist, child killer and most of all importantly cannibal. Born in 1870, Mr. Fish enjoyed spankings with a nail-studded paddles and embedding needles in his groin. On the right, notice the X-ray...

CLOSE UP - X-RAY

INTERCUT shots of Albert Fish

STARTS FRIDAY, APRIL 11TH!

●**WESTWOOD**
Mann Plaza (310) 248-MANN #054
Daily: 12:15 • 2:30 • 5:15 • 8:00 • 10:45

●**HOLLYWOOD**
THX Mann Chinese 6 (323) 777-FILM #059
Daily: 12:40 • 3:00 • 5:30 • 7:50 • 10:10
Fri. & Sat. Late Show: 12:30 am

✱**BEVERLY HILLS**
AMC Beverly Connection (310) 659-5911
Daily: 2:20 • 5:00 • 7:50 • 10:15

✱**UNIVERSAL CITY**
Loews Cineplex Universal Studios Cinema
(800) 555-TELL
Daily: 12:00 • 2:30 • 4:50 • 7:20 • 10:00
Fri. & Sat. Late Show: 12:15 am

●**SANTA MONICA**
THX Mann Criterion 6 (310) 248-MANN #019
Daily: 11:15 • 2:00 • 4:45 • 7:30 • 10:00

✱**WEST LOS ANGELES**
The Bridge Cinema De Lux (310) 568-3375
Daily: 12:45 • 3:00 • 5:15 • 7:30 • 9:45
Fri. & Sat. Late Show: 12:00 am

✱**BALDWIN HILLS**
Magic Theatres at Crenshaw Plaza
(800) 555-TELL
Daily: 11:20 • 2:00 • 4:40 • 7:30 • 10:10

●**AGOURA HILLS**
THX Mann Agoura Hills 8

✱**ALHAMBRA**
Edwards Atlantic Palace 10
(800) 555-TELL

✱**ALISO VIEJO**
Edwards Aliso Viejo 20
(800) 555-TELL

✱**ANAHEIM HILLS**
Edwards Anaheim Hills Festival
(800) 555-TELL

●**ANAHEIM HILLS**
Cinema City Theatres
(714) 970-6700

✱**BAKERSFIELD**
Edwards Bakersfield 14
(800) 555-TELL

●**BAKERSFIELD**
Pacific's Valley Plaza Stadium 16
(661) 833-2200

✱**BREA**
Edwards Brea Stadium 22
(800) 555-TELL

✱**BURBANK**
AMC Burbank 14
(818) 953-9800

✱**CATHEDRAL CITY**
Mary Pickford 14 Cinemas
(760) 328-7100

●**CHATSWORTH**
Pacific's Winnetka Stadium 21
(818) 501-5121

✱**CORONA**
Edwards Big Corona 15
(800) 555-TELL

✱**COVINA**
AMC Covina 30
(626) 974-8600

✱**EL MONTE**
Edwards El Monte 8
(800) 555-TELL

✱**FULLERTON**
AMC Fullerton 20
(714) 992-6000

●**GARDEN GROVE**
Regal Cinemas Garden Grove 16
(714) 534-4777

●**GLENDALE**
THX Mann Theatres at the Exchange
(818) 549-0045

●**GRANADA HILLS**
THX Mann Granada Hills 9
(818) 363-3679

✱**HUNTINGTON BEACH**
Mann Pierside Pavilion 6
(714) 969-3151

✱**IRVINE**
Edwards 21 MegaPlex Cinemas
(800) 555-TELL

✱**JURUPA VALLEY**
Edwards Jurupa Stadium 14
(800) 555-TELL

●**LA HABRA**
Regal Cinemas La Habra Marketplace 16
(562) 690-7469

●**LAKEWOOD**
Pacific's Lakewood Center Stadium 16
(562) 531-9580

LANCASTER
Cinemark Lancaster
(661) 940-1136

✱**LONG BEACH**
AMC Marina Pacifica 12
(562) 435-4AMC

✱**LONG BEACH**
AMC Pine Square 16
(562) 435-4AMC

✱**LONG BEACH**
Edwards Long Beach Stadium 26
(800) 555-TELL

MARINA DEL REY
United Artists Cinemas
(310) 777-FILM #301

●**MORENO VALLEY**
Canyon Springs

●**MURRIETA**
The Movie Experience 17 at California Oaks
(909) 698-7800

●**NORTH HOLLYWOOD**
Century 8 Theatres
(818) 508-6004

✱**NORWALK**
AMC Norwalk 20
(562) 864-5678

✱**ONTARIO**
AMC Ontario Mills 30
(909) 484-3000

✱**ONTARIO**
Edwards Mountain Village Stadium 14 Cinemas
(800) 555-TELL

✱**ONTARIO**
Edwards Ontario 22
(800) 555-TELL

●**ORANGE**
Century Stadium 25
(714) 532-9533

✱**ORANGE**
AMC 30 at the Block
(714) 769-4AMC

PALMDALE
Antelope Valley 10
(661) 267-4940

●**PARAMOUNT**
Bianchi Theatres
(562) 630-SHOW

✱**PASADENA**
AMC Old Pasadena 8
(626) 585-8900

POMONA
Indian Hill Cinema
(909) 469-6550

✱**PUENTE HILLS**
AMC Puente Hills 20
(626) 810-5566

✱**REDONDO BEACH**
AMC Galleria at So. Bay 16
(310) 793-7077

●**SAN BERNARDINO**
CinemaStar Empire 20
(909) 386-7050

✱**SAN LUIS OBISPO**
Fremont
(805) 541-2141

●**SHERMAN OAKS**
Pacific's Galleria Stadium 16
(818) 501-5121

✱**SIMI VALLEY**
Regal Cinemas Civic Center 16
(805) 526-9800

●**SOUTH BAY**
Pacific's Beach Cities Cinema 16
(310) 607-0007

✱**SOUTH GATE**
Edwards South Gate Stadium 20
(800) 555-TELL

●**TEMECULA**
The Movie Experience At Tower Plaza
(909) 698-7800

●**THOUSAND OAKS**
THX Mann Janss Marketplace 9
(805) 374-9656

✱**TORRANCE**
AMC Rolling Hills 20
(310) 289-4AMC

●**VAN NUYS**
Mann Plant 16
(818) 779-0323

●**VENTURA**
Mann Buenaventura
(805) 658-6544

VICTORVILLE
Bear Valley 10
(760) 241-8400

✱**WEST COVINA**
Edwards West Covina 18 at The Lakes
(800) 555-TELL

●**WHITTIER**
Whittier Village
(562) 907-3300

✱Presented in DOLBY

●Presented in DOLBY SR

21 CONTINUED: 21

SPAULDING (CONT'D)
...showing clearly 29 sewing needles inserted in to his groin. Mr. Fish was executed in 1936 at the age of 65.

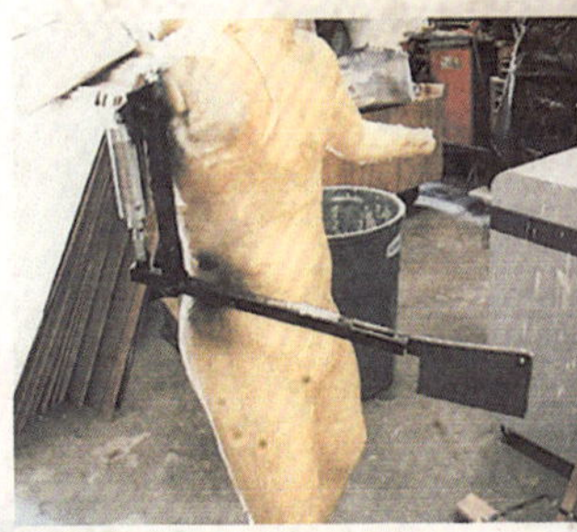

JERRY
I have a question.

SPAULDING
Hold all questions.

Spaulding rolls backwards and continues the tour.

CLOSE UP ON : a dummy face of a grizzly looking old man in hunting attire.

SPAULDING (CONT'D)
To your right. One of our most popular crazies, the psycho of Plainfield, Ed Gein. *

Behind the figure of Gein hangs an inverted corpse of a slain woman.

Mary recoils in disgust, but snaps a photo anyway. *

SPAULDING (CONT'D)
Murderer, cannibal and momma's little bitch boy. Mr. Gein found special pleasure...
(leans closer to Mary)
...in playing with the dead bodies of women, especially their sexual organs. *

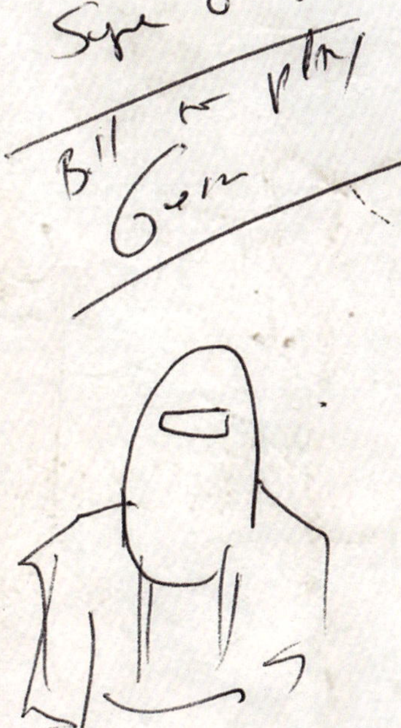

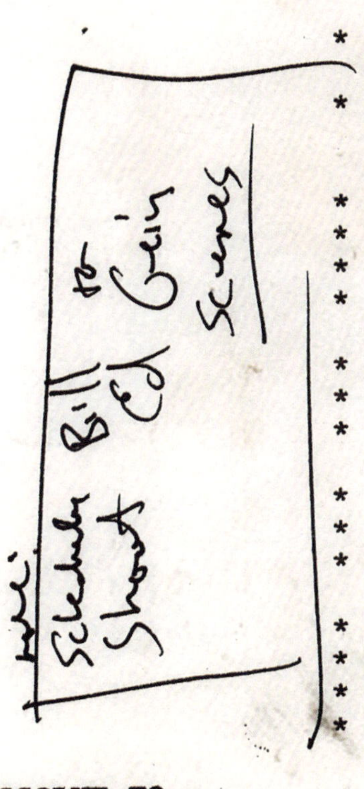

JERRY
Sounds like something Bill is familiar with. *

DENISE
(elbows Jerry)
Will you calm down. *

SPAULDING
He was quite a handy little dandy, fashioning lamp shades, jewelry and a human suit from his victims. *

DISSOLVE TO :

A wax figure of a young man in doctor's scrubs. He is covered in blood.

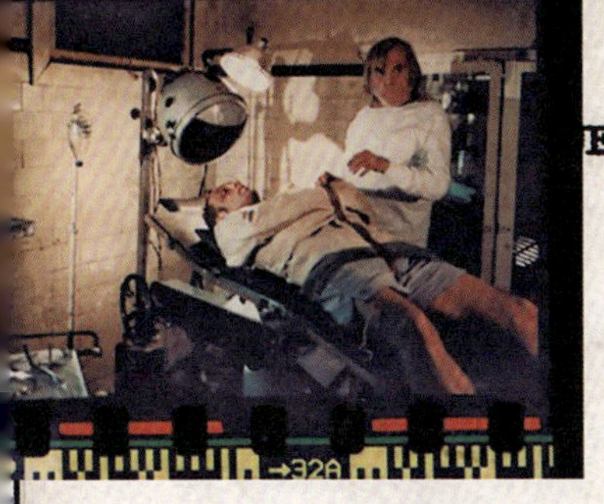

SPAULDING (CONT'D)
And now I would like to introduce a local hero, S.Quentin Quale a.k.a. The Butcher Boy, a.k.a. Nurse Nellie and most famously a.k.a. Dr.Satan.

Another wax figure, of a bloody corpse, JUMPS up.

SPAULDING (CONT'D)
Murderer, torturer and most of all master surgeon. Mr. Quale an intern at Willows State Mental Hospital, nicknamed Weeping Willows for it's never ending cries of pain.

BILL
Is this a true story?

SPAULDING
No, I'm making it up...of course it's true!

BILL
Sorry.

SPAULDING
You made me lose my damn place.

BILL
Something about cries of pain.

SPAULDING
Oh right,..Through primitive brain surgery. Mr. Quale believed he could create a race of superhumans from the mentally ill ~~or so the story goes. His terrifying experiments continued until 1952.~~

FLASH BACK Embassador Hotel

DR. SATAN BASEMENT

Jerry stares fascinated.

SPAULDING (CONT'D)
Mr. Quale was abducted from his cell by ~~members of the victims families.~~ Vigilante justice prevailed and Dr. Satan was taken out and hanged. The next day his body was found to be missing. To this day no sign of Dr. Satan has ever been discovered. But who knows? Maybe he lives next door to you.

KLUNK! A big metal door opens to the outside world.

(CONTINUED)

WRITTEN AND DIRECTED BY ROB ZOMBIE
HOUSE OF 1000 CORPSES
BABY
OTIS
CLOWNFACE
CAPTAIN
MOTHER
AQUALINA
THE FEEGEE MERMAID

21 CONTINUED: 21

SPAULDING (CONT'D)
Please exit through the door.

A21 EXT. SPAULDING'S - NIGHT A21

The kids exit through the mouth of the giant skull.

JERRY
That was bad-ass...
(screaming)
...Dr. Satan.

BILL
It was alright.

MARY
Can we go now?

SLAM! The metal door shuts.

DENISE
I'm gonna call my dad, I'll be right back.

JERRY
OK...
(to Bill)
...what do you mean it was alright?

BILL
It was cool, but it wasn't that great.

JERRY
Dude, you don't have to play it down in front of your chick.

22 EXT. SPAULDING'S - PHONE BOOTH - NIGHT 22

Denise leans against the glass walls of the phone booth. Various flyer are taped to the inside: free kittens, phone sex ads and a missing poster for a girl named KAREN MURPHY. A light rain begins to fall.

Denise puts some change in the phone and dials a number.

A22 EXT. WILLIS HOUSE - NIGHT A22

The camera moves down a quaint quiet little street. We come to rest at modest two-story house. The house is decorated for Halloween.

Parents and their children roam from house to house, trick or treating.

Spaulding Road Sign – "House of 1000 Corpses"

NEXT EXIT

CAPTAIN SPAULDING'S MUSEUM of MONSTERS AND MADMEN

CHICKEN AND GASOLINE

NEXT EXIT
CAPTAIN SPAULDING'S MUSEUM of MONSTERS AND MADMEN
CHICKEN AND GASOLINE
SHERIFF
FRIED CHICKEN AND GASOLINE
SEE THE EVIL BRAIN SURGEON KNOWN AS DOCTOR SATAN
Phone
FUN 4 THE WHOLE

HI ROB!
NOW IF I HAD A
SON, WHAT MORE COULD
I ASK FOR.
Harrison

A22 CONTINUED: A22

We hear the sound of a phone ringing.

23 INT. WILLIS HOUSE - KITCHEN - NIGHT 23

A grey haired man sits at a small table eating a ham sandwich and drinking a beer. This is DONALD WILLIS, Denise's father.

He stands up and walks to the phone hanging on the wall.

MR.WILLIS
Hello...
(brightens up)
...hey Denise... what, what's wrong did you break down.

24 EXT. SPAULDING'S - PHONE BOOTH - NIGHT 24

DENISE
No, nothing like that... yeah, we're gonna be a little late. We stopped for gas at this place called J.T. Spaulding's outside of Ruggsville and it turn into a whole thing, so we're kind of behind schedule. *

25 INT. WILLIS HOUSE - NIGHT 25

MR.WILLIS
Oh yeah, yeah I've driven by that place before. I seem to remember a crabby old bastard in a crummy clown suit running the place.

A25 INT. PHONE BOOTH - NIGHT A25

DENISE
Yeah, well he's still here. I think him and Jerry are fast becoming buddies, you know Jerry... yeah, he's gotta see everything... yeah, I know... thinks there's some unsolved mystery around every corner.

B25 INT. WILLIS HOUSE - NIGHT B25

MR.WILLIS
Well, don't take to long the kids are already knocking down the door demanding their sugar fix... I know, I know I forgot to mention that Halloween falls on a school night, so they're trick or treating tonight... I got the joint decked out this year, built a graveyard
(MORE)

PERIENCE
EAL LIFE
ORROR
NOT
FOR
TOUR
MONSTERS
AND
MADMEN
FUN 4
THE WHOLE
FAMILY

ALBERT FISH

B25 CONTINUED: B25

MR.WILLIS (cont'd)
in the front yard like when you were a kid...and those damn McKluski kids TP'd the whole damn street again.

C25 EXT. SPAULDING'S - PHONE BOOTH - NIGHT C25

DENISE
Well, hopefully I can move things along here and make up the lost time by...
(monster truck voice)
...puttin' the pedal to the metal all the way home, baby... yes, Dad I'm kidding.

Your left hand shows your past
your right hand shows your future

D25 OMIT D25

26 EXT. CAR - NIGHT 26

Bill, Jerry and Mary wait for Denise.

JERRY
(to Bill)
I'm gonna go ask him, dude. I totally think its worth it.

MARY
Aw, come on Jerry. We've gotten all we're gonna get out this place.

JERRY
Was I talkig to you?

MARY
(gives him the finger)
Eat me.

JERRY
You wish.

BILL
Come on, we're late enough as it is. already and it's starting to rain.

JERRY
Shit, it is only sprinkling and it's worth the trouble. Hold on for two seconds.

Jerry goes back inside, he turns and yells to Mary.

(CONTINUED)

insert 7 O'clock News —

I'm Lance Brockwell and this is the Seven O'clock News. And our top story tonight. Investigators still have no leads in the strange disappearance of the five cheerleaders from Russellville High School. Connie Thompson, Karen Murphy, Ann Cole

Valerie Green, Dawn Baker were last seen 4 days ago leaving a football game

Lance Brockwell

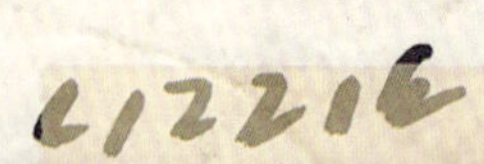

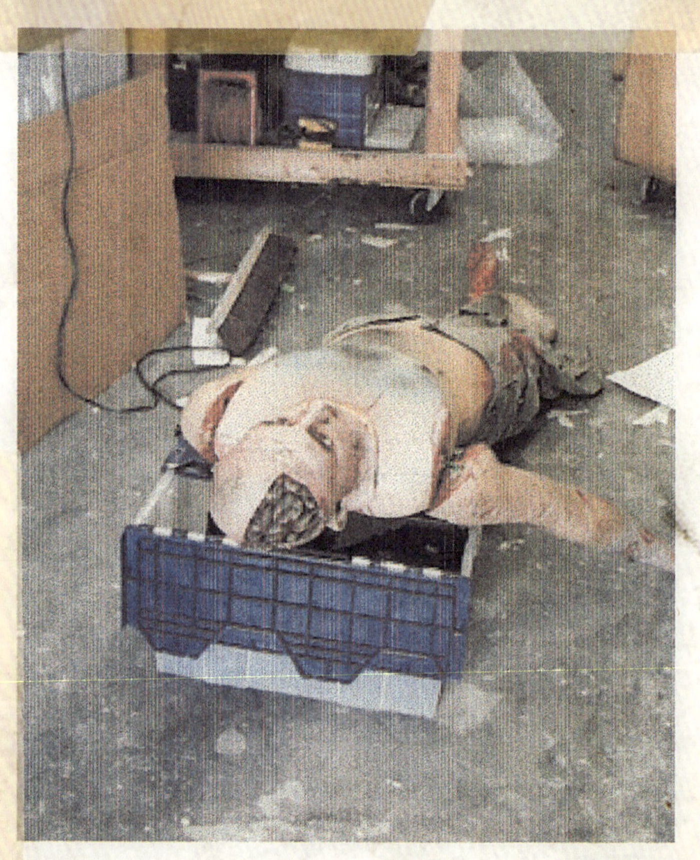

LIZZIES FATHER

26 CONTINUED: 26

JERRY (cont'd)
Hey, don't forget to get pictures of the outside.

She flips him off again.

27 INT. PHONE BOOTH - NIGHT 27

Jerry knocks on the glass as he passes. Denise waves as he walks by.

DENISE
Yeah so... OK, expect us more around eleven or so. OK yeah, I will... love you too, bye.

She hangs up the phone, opens the doors and heads back to the car.

28 INT. SPAULDING'S - NIGHT 28

JERRY
I know it seems stupid, but I really want to see this tree.

SPAULDING
Do yourself a favor kid, forget about it.

JERRY
Aw, come on. I live for this shit.

SPAULDING
OK, alright I'll draw you a map, but I still say it is a waste of time.

JERRY
Great.

29 INT. CAR. - NIGHT 29

Through the window we see Jerry talking to Spaulding. Spaulding draws a map, explaining as he draws.

Mary is taking pictures of the exterior of Spaulding's.

BILL
Geez, he never gets tired does he.

DENISE
Never. I swear to God he never sleeps, he goes to bed after me, wakes up before me. He's always working on 10.

(CONTINUED)

NO TURNING BACK!

29 CONTINUED: 29

BILL *
Maybe he's a cyborg.. *

DENISE
Here he comes my little mechanical boy *
now. *

Jerry comes bouncing out towards the car. He is holding a map *
and a box of chicken.

Insert mangler as Russel MISSING posters

JERRY
You guys are going to thank me for this *
one! Let's roll, good buddy. We got *
ourselves a convoy. *

BILL
Hey Mary, let's go.

MARY
(rolling her eyes)
Jesus, make up your mind.

DENISE
Ugh, what's that smell.

JERRY
Fried chicken.
(holds up a drumstick)
Anybody want some.

No one responds.

30 EXT. WOODS - DAY

An old man, FARMER MAILHOUSE and his his wife ALICE stare *
directly into the camera.

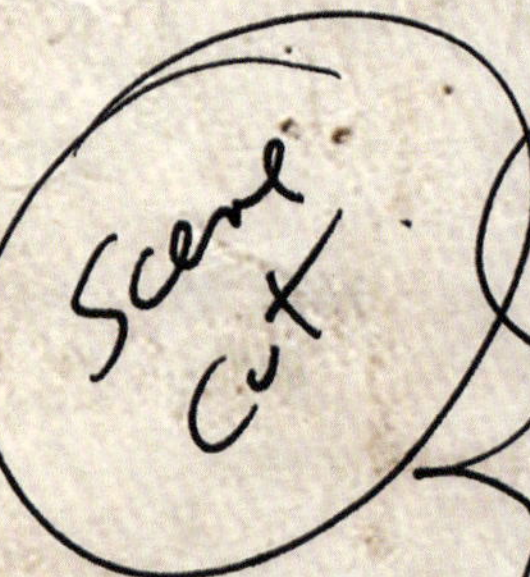

FARMER *
I don't know where that skunk ape sleeps.
Maybe in the trees and all... all I know
is he eats squirrels to survive and he
had impure relations with my wife.

ALICE *
That's true. He performed lurid acts upon
me and my person while my husband Russell
was a fix'n to our hound Clarence.

FARMER *
He leaves a trail behind himmthat smells *
like a skunk. *

30 CONTINUED:

ALICE
That's also true.

FARMER
If I see that thing again...I'm a gonna kill that skunk ape.

ALICE
It looked just like that chubby fella from McHale's Navy... Ernie Borgnine.

FARMER
Hold up the picture.

Alice holds up a pencil sketch of a Bigfoot like creature and newspaper photo of Ernest Borgnine.

31 EXT. COUNTRY ROAD - NIGHT 31

Bill's car moves pass empty farmlands. A HEAVIER RAIN is now falling.

32 INT. CAR. - NIGHT 32

Jerry directs Bill from Spaulding's hand-drawn map.

JERRY
Keep straight on this road here...I think.

BILL
You think...how much further is it?

JERRY
I'm not exactly sure...it looks pretty close. Did we pass an abandoned school bus yet?

BILL
I don't know, I can't make out shit.

Mary and Denise sit bundled up in blankets.

MARY
Let's just skip it. It is probably nothing anyway.

DENISE
Aw, Christ Jerry. Bill is right, we can't see anything now, it's too dark.

MARY
Let's just forget it.

(CONTINUED)

House of 1000 Corpses

verse She got a Corpse under her bed

1 She kept her for but now her Dead

Her mum said "come feed Desire"

Her Sister Said "Hey throw him in the fire"

This is the House

Its Come on in

This is the House

built on SIN

This is the house

Nobody Lives

This is the House - get what ya give

Chorus

Now your lying on the floor

Fear your can't take my love

3 The Deadly laugh in your face

Give one awful taste

→ Chorus

I cut the flesh on melting blood

2 Fresh skin is what I need

I let it dry out in the wind

Were all your organs dead no good

→ Chorus

Baby
Firefly

Baby
#plays
innocent but
most crazy of all.
s the Bait to
me victims to
house. Constantly
t adds with otts
other/ sister fights.
protects They from
he world. of
as dreams of
stardum.

32 CONTINUED: 32

JERRY
Come on, we need something like this. It could be the real deal.

DENISE
Maybe we can hit it on the way back?

JERRY
It's too far out of the way to come back to.

BILL
What's that?

Through the windshield we see a LONE FIGURE hitchhiking by the side of the road. It is a girl, BABY, 27, in a worn cowboy hat and long fur coat. She holds a small, ratty umbrella.

JERRY
It's hitchhiker.

BILL
Way out here?

MARY
Well, don't even think about playing the good samaritan, there's way too many psychos wandering loose these days.

BILL
(looking closer)
It's a girl.

JERRY
Hey, maybe she knows where this is?

DENISE
(sarcastically)
That seems likely.

MARY
Should we stop?

BILL
We can't leave her out here in the rain... maybe we can just drop her at the next rest area.

MARY
She looks like a freak.

32 CONTINUED: 32

DENISE
Stick her in the front, if you want to pick her up so bad. She's soaked.

~~MARY~~
~~She looks like she stinks.~~

~~BILL~~
~~(imitating Mary)~~
~~She looks like she stinks.~~

~~JERRY~~
~~(makes cat noises)~~
~~Catfight, catfight.~~

~~DENISE~~
~~Hardy har, har.~~

The car pulls over and Baby jumps in. The car moves off.

33 INT. CAR - NIGHT 33

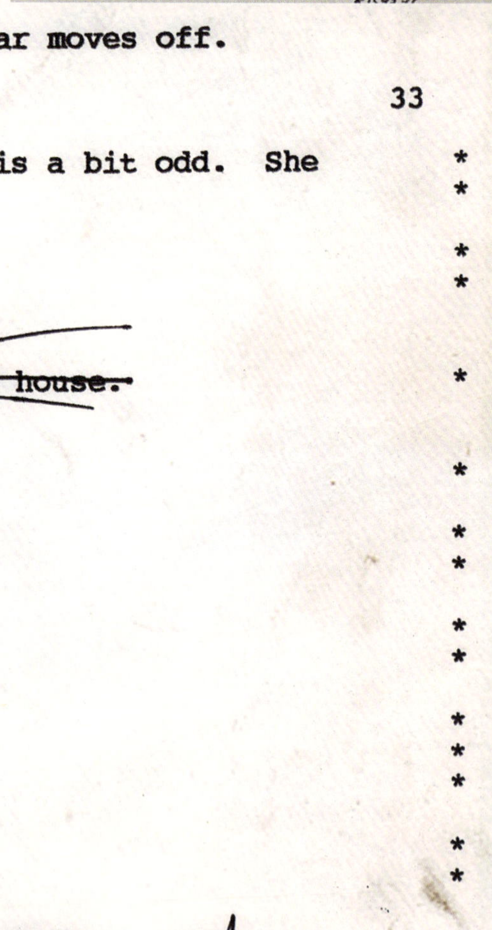

Once inside the car they see that the girl is a bit odd. She sits silent. *

BILL *
Hey, where ya headed? *

BABY
Aw, I was going home ~~to my mama's house.~~ *

JERRY
Where's that? *

note: need music cue

BABY *
Couple more miles up the road. *

JERRY *
So you live around here? *

BABY *
Yeah. *

JERRY *
Hey, you might know... *
(shows her the map)
... you know where this tree is at? ~~It's an old hanging tree from..~~

The Baby PERKS UP at the mention of the tree.

BABY
Yeah, I know where that is, it's right by my house. ~~It Dr. Satan's tree.~~ I can show ya.

Mary Morphs Fuck You at Jerry

JERRY
Really,
(He turns and smirks at Mary)
...so it's a really a real thing.

BABY
Yeah, it's a real tree. I used to have all kinds a fun out there. But, you won't find it without me.

BILL
Why's that?

BABY
Outsider can't find no Deadwood.

JERRY
Deadwood is that what it's called? Cool, will you show us?

BABY
Maybe...hey you know what word I hate?

JERRY
What?

BABY
Cone.

JERRY
Huh... what cone?

BABY
Any cone, yeah...
(looking out the window)
I hate that word... sounds ugly.

JERRY
I always hating saying the word cheese, every time ya get your picture taken some dick yells out smile say cheese, so weak.

BABY
(whispering)
I know I hate Swiss cheese, the holes make me nervous.

HOUSE OF 1000 CORPSES
THERE'S NO TURNING BACK!
A FILM BY ROB ZOMBIE

33 CONTINUED: 33

JERRY
(whispering)
Why are we whispering?

BABY
I don't know.

BILL
What about the tree.

BABY
What tree?

MARY
This is crazy. She don't know nothing.

Baby turns her attention toward Mary.

BABY
Oh, I know. I'll show you where it's at, sweetie.

Insert sister's speech
BABY
Whatever you need to do you do it. There is no wrong.
If someone needs to be killed ya kill'em
THAT'S THE WAY

MARY
Oh, really.

JERRY
Cool.

BILL
Which way?

BABY
Go straight up about another mile... then I'll show ya what to do...it ain't far from here.

34 INT.- MENTAL HOSPITAL 34

The camera FLOATS through the hallways of the Peabody Mental Institution. It is HALLOWEEN.

PATIENTS wander the stark halls dressed in hospital gowns and cheap plastic masks. Some are laughing, some are screaming.

We move into a private room. Where we see a DOCTOR SATAN completely covered except for his eyes, hovering over a BOUND and GAGGED PATIENT.

We move off the doctor to a crayon child's DRAWING of a JACK-O'- LANTERN. Tortured screams fill the room.

BABY wardrobe fitting

D/N
PAGES
LOCATION
nk Pussy Cat Liquors
ying booze
aulding's
nt bust the crapper
aulding's
is is a stick up
N2
17/8
24/8
2
East 145th Street & Ave Q
Palmdale ,Calif
Sc. 9 If Time P
No Cove
Rehearsal
Rehearsa
Rehearsa
Rehearsa
ain
e Dodd
eg Brazze
OSPHERE / STA
t,Emily
n Photo Dbl.
Plumber butt
Bedroom
#3

35 EXT. CHERRYPICKER RD.- WOODS - NIGHT 35

From a STRANGER'S POV we see the car ~~STRUGGLING down a dirt road.~~

36 INT. CAR - SAME 36

Everyone rides in silence, music plays on the radio.

The song ends and a NEWS REPORTER comes on.

NEWS REPORTER
(V.O.)
This WJRC News at the top of the hour... Investigators in Clairemont County are no closer to identifying the body of a young woman found crucified to the doors of St. Mary's Church yesterday morning.

Baby lights up a cigarette and takes a drag.

MARY
Excuse me, could you not smoke in here.

Baby puts out the cigarette in the palm of her hand. *

NEWS REPORTER *
Local police and State Officials have *
released this report... *

JERRY
What's that?

BILL
I don't know. Looks like some kind of animal.

Bill stops the car.

37 EXT. CHERRYPICKER RD. - WOODS- NIGHT 37

Sitting dead center in the middle of the road is a HUMONGOUS DOG. The dog stares straight ahead. Long strands of drool hang from its mouth to the ground.

38 INT. CAR - NIGHT

MARY
Why are we stopping?

BILL
There's a dog in the road.

(CONTINUED)

Hey R.W.
I SAY, this picture
is going to be
FIRST cabin all The
WAY! STERLING, I SAY
But Seriously –
you suck This
film sucks ASS
AND I cant WAIT
TO see you in
Hell!! Die!!!!
But Seriously –
4th period WAS such a blast
with you & me & Patty Pee Pee
Pants! HAVE A ROCKIN summer!
But Seriously,
I Think I'm in LOVE w/ you
–RAINN

38 CONTINUED: 38

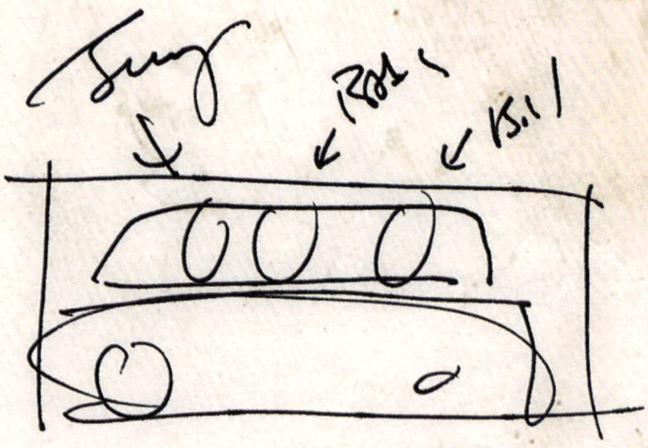

DENISE
Honk at him. Scare him.

BILL
(honking horn)
He won't move.

MARY
Go around him.

BILL
There's not enough room.

MARY
Then run him over, he'll move.

BABY
No! He's one of God's creature, he can help it if he's dumb... I'm just crazy about animals.

MARY
(to Denise)
The animals have got nothing to do with it.

39 EXT. STRANGER'S POV - SAME 39

A gun barrel is raised an we are looking through the sight at the car. Pop! Pop! Pop! The GUN fires THREE SHOTS at the car's rear tire.

The stranger whistles and the dog moves to the side of the road.

40 INT. CAR - NIGHT 40

The SOUND of the heavy rain MASKS the gunshots.

BILL
Hey, he moved.

MARY
Let's get going before that thing tries to eat the car or something.

As the car moves past, Denise stares at the dog sitting calmly to the side of the road. The dog blankly stares back at her.

(CONTINUED)

Rob-
What can I say? I think
the absolute world of you. I can unequivocally say
that this—from start to finish—has been my
favorite project I've ever worked on. My only
fear is that it doesn't get any better than this.
And that is due to this amazing group of people
you have brought together and the tone you have
set as director. You are immensely talented—I
look forward to the great things you will do
in the future. Thank you so much for letting
me be part of this one. I've loved every minute
of it. w/love & respect,
Jennifer Jostyn
HEEEEEEY! Why don't we just goooo...

40 CONTINUED: 40

JERRY
That reminds me of a film I saw once of a guy who got out of his car at Lion Country Safari to take a picture of a lion cub and got eaten by the lions.

BILL
O' yeah, I heard about that. I always thought it was bullshit.

JERRY
No... yeah, they ripped him to pieces while his family watched from the car. The wife is screaming, the kids are crying. Some dude in another car filmed the whole thing.

BABY
I'd like to see that.

MARY
Nice.

JERRY
The lions were totally covered in this guy's blood... I think they ate his face off, tore open his rib cage open, pulled his legs off... it was a wild scene.

BABY
Things like that get a lot bloodier than ya think.

Without warning the car lunges to one side.

JERRY
What was that?

BILL
Fuck. I think we blew a tired.

MARY
Don't even say it .

DENISE
You got to be fucking joking.

MARY
God damn it, I knew this witch-hunt was fucking bullshit.

(CONTINUED)

Rufus
Huge
Backwoods brute.
Keeps the winning machines running.
The muscle behind the whims of Otis.
Lives among the graveyard of wrecked cars and stolen trucks.
A wanderer.
Spends most nights in the woods.
Always the trigger man for Baby's prey.
MACK
Guts Glory
Rufus Firefly
clothes
mechanic gear
Hunting gear mix with animal skins and other gathered objects
Sometimes wear clothes of victims

40 CONTINUED: 40

BILL
OK, let's relax. I'll check it, maybe I'm wrong. Don't everybody freak out just yet.

JERRY
I'll help ya.

BILL
(sarcastic)
Gee, ya think it wouldn't be too much trouble.

41 EXT. CHERRYPICKER ROAD - WOODS - NIGHT 41

Bill and Jerry stare down at the blown tire sunk in the mud.

BILL
I hope you fixed the spare like I asked ya.

JERRY
Yeah, I fixed it. Well, I ain't ... um, I can't remember. I think I took it out to fit the bags and forgot to put it back.

BILL
Jesus Christ, Jerry.

JERRY
Well, technically I did what ya said.

BILL
You're a real piece of work. *

JERRY *
I know. *

Bill stares at Jerry in disbelief.

42 INT. CAR - NIGHT 42

Baby is leaning on her chin staring at Mary and Denise. The car radio plays in the background.

MARY
Can I help you with something?

BABY
I was just wondering.

MARY
Wondering what?

(CONTINUED)

HOUSE
1000
CORPSES

42 CONTINUED: 42

BABY
You girls like eat pie? *

MARY
What?

DENISE *
Yeah, I guess so. *

BABY
I knew it. *

MARY *
Oh, really? *

BABY *
Yeah, I knew you were a couple of queers *
the second I laid eyes on you. *

DENISE *
Excuse me? *

MARY *
Do you believe this fucking girl?

BABY
(turning her attention to Mary)
You especially got a pissy look about *
you... you must be a real pussy licking *
bitch.

Denise tries to QUICKLY defuse the situation.

DENISE
No. No pussy licking here but, thanks for
your concern.

Bill and Jerry slide back into the car.

BABY *
Hey, how'd it go? *

BILL
Well, I got some bad news and some bad
news.

BABY *
Uh-oh. *

MARY
What?

(CONTINUED)

JERRY
(fake Scottish accent)
Tire's fucking gone crap on us, man.
There's no saving it now.

BILL
And the spare is safely sitting in
Jerry's garage.

DENISE
For fucking sake Jerry, what the fuck are
we gonna do? *

JERRY *
(scottish accent) *
I can't say as if I rightly know, me *
ladies. *

Baby starts laughing.

MARY
What the hell are you laughing about?

BABY
I just pictured a monkey swinging from *
your tire. *

MARY
Oh, wonderful.
(muttering to herself)
Fucking psycho.

BILL
I guess I'll try to back it out on the
rim... at least to the main road.

BABY
If you keep going straight you can get
back on the interstate... it's easier.

MARY
Just back up.

JERRY
I think we should go straight. I mean we
known for a fact there ain't nothing back
that way, right?

BABY
Oh wait! I love this song!

Baby reaches over and TURNS UP the VOLUME. She loudly sings
along with the song.

(CONTINUED)

100 TH MAG

42 CONTINUED: 42

BILL
Fine. I'll go straight.

MARY
What!

BILL
(over the loud music)
Fine! I'll go straight!

The car moves forward. After about fifty yards the car HITS something hard and gets stuck in a deep mud bog.

BILL (CONT'D)
Fuck ! We are fucked !

DENISE
Turn that fucking radio off!

Baby
I love this song.

Bill shuts off the radio.

DENISE (CONT'D)
Now what are we gonna do?

BABY
We can walk to my house from here. *

DENISE *
What? *

BABY
Yeah, my brother's got a towtruck, he can come get your car.

A silence falls over the car.

MARY
I think I'm going fucking crazy.

DENISE
I can't believe...

BILL
OK, whatever. Let's go get your brother's truck. Faster we get the truck, faster we get out off here.

BABY
OK

JERRY
I'll go. It's my fault.

Jerry
I'll go it's my fault

Bill
forget it
I'm going

(CONTINUED)

HOUSE OF
1000 CORPSES

43 CONTINUED: 43

RADIO V.O.

Turning now to the news: local authorities still have no leads in the mystery disappearance of 5 cheerleaders from Nyssaville. The girls were last seen leaving a cheering competition.

... W.C. FIELDS and CLARK

...S BUNNY, 55, comes into
... gown with feathers in

...tion)
...e in the *
...ome you to *

... for *

...er.

44 I... 44

Ti... ...nd everything, the
wa... ...nt hand prints of movie
gre... Badly sculpted statues of
MAR... ...O MARX and JOHN WAYNE stand in the
cor...

Dead center is a small puppet show stage.

MISS BUNNY
This is where the magic happens, legends *
spring to life before your eyes. *

CLOSE UP - SQUIRREL

A stuffed squirrel dressed in a gray skirt and jacket, a tilted hat sits atop its head.

MISS BUNNY
(holding up squirrel)
This Jenny, she is our resident Ingrid Bergman.

Miss Bunny picks up a stuffed white cat wearing a brown trench coat.

MISS BUNNY (CONT'D)
This is Ronald J. Perrywinckle... our Humphrey Bogart... today we'll be doing a scene from Casablanca.

Miss Bunny begins to make the dead animal puppets interact. She provides their voices.

Cut

To Rob
With Love
Joanne Carman

Otis Speech

why you ask? why is not the question... how? now that is a question worth examining. how could I being born of such conventional stock arrive a leader of the rebellion? An ~~[illegible]~~ Escapist from a Conformist world.. destined to find happiness only in that which can not be explained. I brought you here for a reason. ~~The reason being that I~~

But unfortunately you and your sentimental minds me no good. My Brain is frozen.. LOCKED!! ~~I have~~

I have to Break free from the calm of mechanical reproduction, are you Tired of [illegible] dying on the surface .. in [illegible]... [illegible] fuck it.

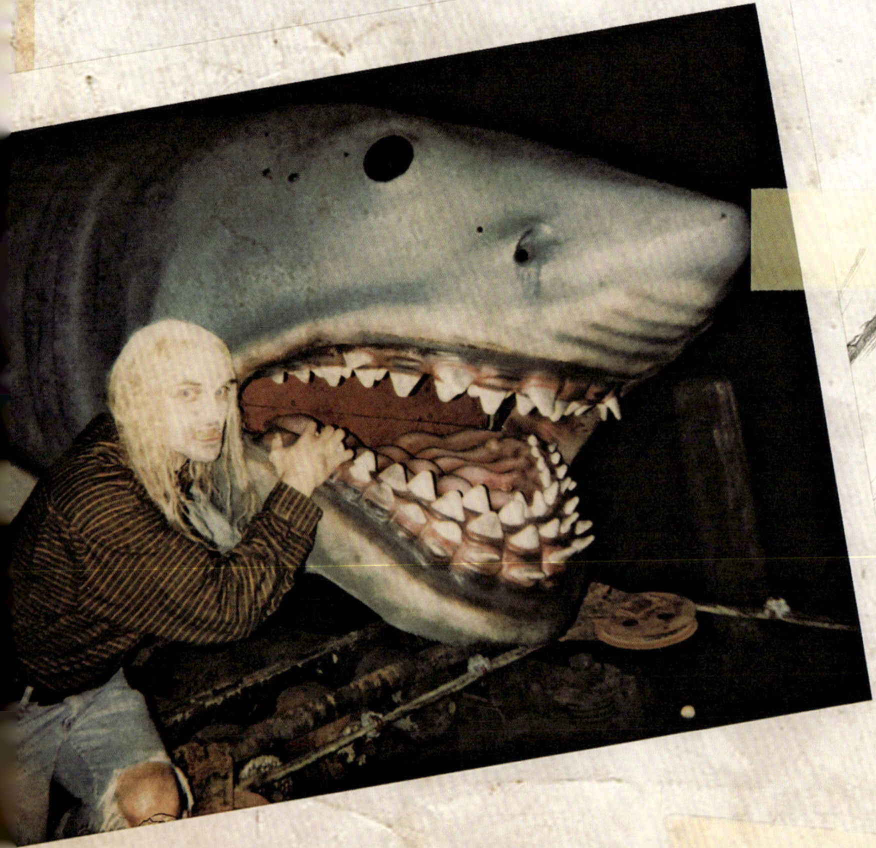

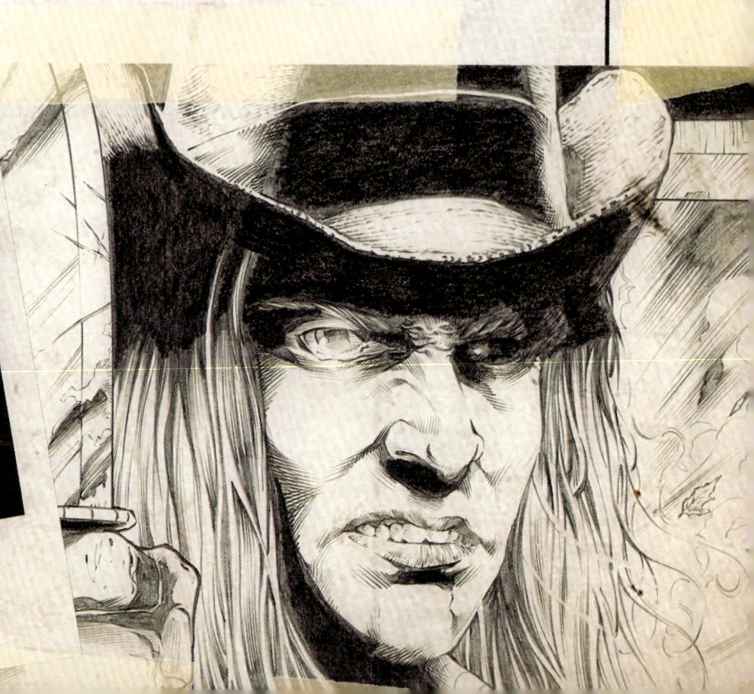

STAY OUT

CONTINUED:

HUMPHREY CAT
If that plane leaves the ground and you're not with him you'll regret it...maybe not today, maybe not tomorrow but soon and for the rest of your life.

INGRID SQUIRREL
But what about us?

HUMPHREY CAT
We'll always have Paris, we didn't have, we lost it... until you came to Casablanca. We got it back last night.

INGRID SQUIRREL
When I said I would never leave you.

HUMPHREY CAT
And you never will.

45 EXT. WOODS - NIGHT 45

A single flashlight beam cuts through the darkness of the dense woods. Bill stumbles behind Baby, she is clearly in her element.

BILL
How much further?

BABY
Almost there... are you in hurry or something?

BILL
Well, yeah kind of.

A45 EXT. CAR - NIGHT A45 *

Bill's car sits in the road. Rain purs down, inside a single light burns. *
*

DENISE *
Fuck, it's freezing. This really sucks. *

JERRY *
Hey, listen to this...I think I found *
something related to our Dr. Satan. *

DENISE *
Since when did he become our Dr. Satan? *

WRITTEN AND DIRECTED
BY ROB ZOMBIE
HOUSE
OF
1000
CORPSES

46 INT. CAR - NIGHT 46

Jerry is stretched out across the front seat, reading a book on Freak Shows. Denise and Mary sit in the back curled up under layers of blankets and clothes.

JERRY *
Huh, listen...in this book there a chapter called Self Made Freaks about how people would mutilate themselves in order to work in a freak show. It mostly talks about tattooed people and wild men of Borneo and shit like that, but there is one mention of a single case where a woman was suspected of having her arms removed on purpose in order to become a arm-less wonder. *

DENISE
Yeah, so how does that fit with the story of four morons with a flat tire looking for a dead tree.

JERRY
It says, "records show that Ellie Thompson was born in 1914 of normal physical stature and lived a life of normal bearings, until such time that she was placed in the care of the Willows County Mental Facility."

DENISE
So.

JERRY
Now she was put in the nuthouse in 1930 at the age of 16.

DENISE
Why?

JERRY
(scanning the book)
Blah, blah, blah... it doesn't say, but she was released sometime in 1937, only reappear as Ellie Bogdan, the arm-less wonder. Says she," crisscrossed the United States constantly in carnivals and freak show until her death in 1946."

DENISE
Yeah, so? *

(CONTINUED)

AN UNSPEAKABLE HORROR

46 CONTINUED: 46

JERRY
These dates perfectly correspond with the time frame of our beloved Dr.Satan working at the looney bin. I'll bet he amputated her arms.

DENISE
So what, Jerry? *

JERRY
I don't know I just thought it was interesting, Denise. *

DENISE
You know what Jerry, at this point who *
really cares? *

JERRY
I don't...
(to himself)
... I just thought it was weird.

MARY
(bursting in)
God damn it, I must be fucking crazy to let him go off with that crazy fucking bitch.

JERRY
Huh?

MARY
That stupid hillbilly slut.

JERRY
Oh, don't blow everything out of proportion.

MARY
You didn't see the look she threw me. She's up to something.

DENISE
Yeah, Jerry, she said some pretty weird shit to us. *

JERRY
When?

DENISE
When you where outside with Bill.

(CONTINUED)

PANAVISION
PANAFLEX

46 CONTINUED: 46

MARY
She said we look like pussy-lickers or
some shit like that.

DENISE
Yeah, she said we looked queer.

JERRY
That's funny, me and Bill wer just saying
the same thing.

DENISE
(smacking the back of Jerry's
head)
Get serious, this isn't funny anymore.

JERRY
Aw, get over it, she's just some dopey
redneck, she ain't smart enough to be up
to nothing... chicks.

47 EXT. FARMHOUSE - NIGHT 47

An old Gothic FARMHOUSE stands atop a hill at the end of long sloping dirtroad. SCARECROWS with pumpkin heads hang CRUCIFIED on crosses lining the drive. Everything is severely overgrown.

Bill and Baby enter the gates of a the FARM, they walk up the main drive.

Baby runs forward and begins jumping around in the huge mud puddles, then runs up onto the front porch of the old house.

The front of the house is covered with strange junk art. Hundreds of dolls faces are nailed to the walls.

BABY
These are all my dolls. I use to like to
chop their heads off and stick'em on the
wall

BILL
Great.

Broken bottles and cans are cemented together in weird HUMAN FIGURES, ANIMAL SKINS are stretched over bone armatures form a makeshift roof.

Glowing down from the upper windows are grinning JACK-O'-LANTERNS.

(CONTINUED)

HOUSE OF
1000 CORPSES

Blue 05/05/2000

47 CONTINUED:

BABY (CONT'D)
The door's locked. I'll gotta go around... wait here.

BILL
OK.

Baby RUNS OFF around the side of the house.

Bill stands looking off into the distance at the desolate farm grounds. The rain continues to hammer down.

From BOLL'S POV, we see a silhouette of a LONE FIGURE can be seen walking in the distance. The shape of a large dog follows behind him.

Bill JUMPS, startled by the sound of the heavy front door opening.

BILL (CONT'D)
Christ, you scared the shit out of me.

BABY
Aw, you ain't seen nothing yet.

BILL
Is your brother ready to go.

BABY
Oh... yeah, he already left. We'll wait inside, come on.

BILL
He left!

BABY
Yeah, come on and get toasty.

Baby GRABS Bill by the arm and pulls him into the house. The door slams heavy iron door slams shut.

48 INT. CAR - SAME 48

Denise and Mary sit facing one another playing cards. Mary deals the from a deck.

Jerry naps in the front seat.

MARY
How long has it been?

DENISE
I don't know... about half an hour.

(CONTINUED)

48 CONTINUED: 48

A metal KLANG is faintly heard.

MARY
What was that?

DENISE
What? I didn't hear anything.

MARY
Wait... quiet. Turn off the radio.

Mary reaches over the front seat and turns off the radio.

DENISE
Now.. listen.

They sit in silence.

MARY
I don't hear anything.

DENISE
(whispering)
Shhhhhh, quiet.

MARY
I still don't.

DENISE
Turn on the headlights. See if anything is out there.

Mary turns on the headlights. Denise lets out a bloodcurdling SCREAM. Jerry bolts up.

JERRY
What...what!

Standing dead center in the road is the GIANT SHAPE of a MAN holding a heavy chain with a huge hook on the end. This is RUFUS. *
*

MARY
Lock the doors... quick, quick.

Everybody scrambles to lock the doors. Rufus walks toward the car. *
*

DENISE
Holy fuck, holy fuck, holy fuck.

On closer inspection, Jerry notices the chain is attached to the back off a TOWTRUCK.

(CONTINUED)

Rob
Thanks for the Opportunity.
I have had a great time.
It's going to be a hit.
Rufus

48 CONTINUED: 48

JERRY
Hold on, hold on! Everybody calm down!
It's the towtruck guy.

MARY
What!

DENISE
Jesus Christ.

MARY
I think I'm gonna have a fucking heart attack.

JERRY
(Scottish accent)
Ok lassies, I think it's time you get to gripping reality.

MARY
Enough with the stupid voices.

Rufus attaches the chain to the car and begins raising it with his truck. *

A SIGN on the side of the truck reads FIREFLY TOWING.

DISSOLVE TO :

49 CLOSE -UP TV SCREEN 49

We are watching a scene from THE OLD DARK HOUSE. GLORIA STUART, RAYMOND MASSEY and MELVYN DOUGLAS are standing in the rain pounding on a huge wooden door.

GLORIA STUART
Knock again louder.

MELVYN DOUGLAS
I should of thought that was loud enough to wake the dead...that's an idea.

RAYMOND MASSEY
What is?

MELVYN DOUGLAS
Wouldn't it be dramatic, supposing the people inside were dead. All stretch out with the lights quietly burning about them.

GLORIA STUART
I'm sure it would be very amusing.

49 CONTINUED: 49

We pull back from the TV to see Bill's clothes drying by the fireplace. Bill, now wearing overalls and a flannel shirt, is sitting on a old over stuffed sofa.

BILL
So, you live here alone... I mean with just your brother?

BABY
(speaking from the kitchen as she passes by the window)
No. There's a bunch a us 'round somewhere... I think Mammas sleepin'. She sleeps alot, now... do you want marshmallows *

BILL
Um, yeah sure, I guess.

Baby enters the room carrying a small tray with two mugs of hot chocolate. She is dressed in a pair of cut off thermal under wear and tiny T-shirt.

BABY
You've got to have the marshmallows, that's what makes it fun.

BILL
Yeah, I guess.

BABY
You sure do a lot of guessing.

Baby sets down the tray, making sure to bend over close to Bill. She hands him his drink and sits down next to him.

BILL
Thank you.

BABY
You're welcome.

BABY moves closer to Bill, he begins to get nervous.

BILL
Hey, um...
(pointing to the mounted animal head over the fireplace)
... wow, he must of been going really fast to smash through that wall. *

49 CONTINUED: 49

BABY *
You sure are silly for a guy with *
glasses...I like that. *

Baby takes off Bill's glasses and puts them on. *

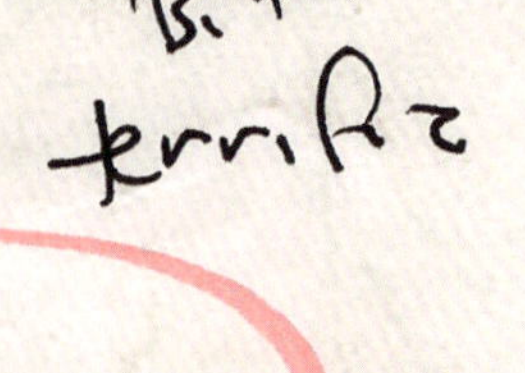

BABY (cont'd) *
How do I look?. *

BILL
(sipping his drink)
Cute...mmmm, this is tasty. *

BABY
(scoops out some marshmallow
with her finger)
Ain't the only thing tasty in this house.
(licks it off)

BILL
I wonder what time it is. Seems kind of
late.

BABY
Don't worry, sugar. It ain't past my
bedtime... are you flirting with me?

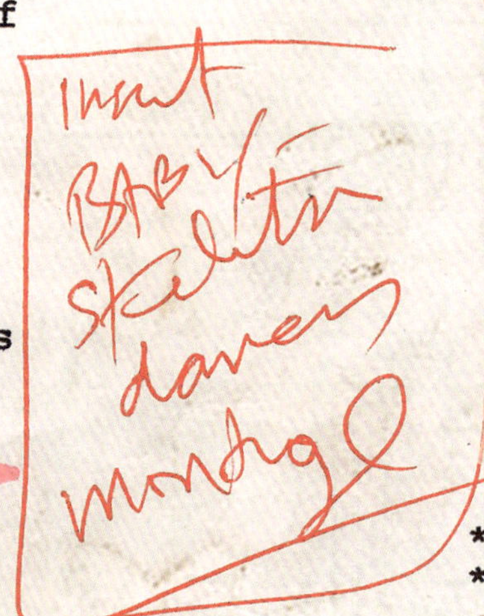

BILL
What? No, I'm was worried that... I was
just wondering what's taking so long.

BABY
Oh. Maybe R.J. got into a crash and
killed everybody and their dead bodies *
are spread all over the road? *

BILL
That's not something to joke about.

BABY
(rolls her eyes)
Ok, sorry... maybe the Great Pumpkin
ate'em up.

Finally, the SOUND OF A TRUCK pulling up can be HEARD. The *
truck's taillights spill through the livingroom window. *

Bill jumps up and goes to the window.

BILL
Hey, great they're back.

49 CONTINUED: 49

BABY
(sarcastically)
Whoopie fucking doo.

50 TV SCREEN -SAME 50

On the B+W screen we see DR. WOLFENSTEIN, a local horror movie host. He looks like a cross between the WOLFMAN and LON CHANEY in LONDON AFTER MIDNIGHT.

DR. WOLFENSTEIN
(sounds like Wolfman Jack)
Aaaahooooh, the Doctor is in! Don't move, don't scream. Stay tuned for more creature craziness from channel 68's Halloween eve movie marathon. I'm your host... your ghost host with the most, baby... Dr. Wolfenstein and will be with you until the end. Aaaaaaahooooooh!

51 EXT. FARMHOUSE - NIGHT 51

Bill stands on the front porch watching, as the truck roughly jerks the car to a stop.

Jerry jumps out, opens the back door and helps Denise.

JERRY
(looking at Bill)
Hey, nice outfit Billy Bob.

DENISE
Thanks for coming to get us. Little brother almost scared us to death.

JERRY
(quietly to Bill as he passes)
Dude, your chicks' a little high strung.

Mary is the last one out of the car. *

Her look says it all as she walks by Bill. *

MARY *
Hi. *

Bill turns to her, speechless, she slams the door in his *
face. *

(CONTINUED)

HOUSE
OF

51 CONTINUED: 51

BILL
Mary, I'm sorry but he left without me.
Mary... come on you don't think I'd leave
you stranded out there.

52 INT. FARMHOUSE - NIGHT 52

Everyone stands around at the fireplace trying to dry off.

DENISE
Look. I gotta call my Dad and tell him
we're gonna be late. Can I use your
phone.

Baby sits silently watching TV.

DENISE (CONT'D)
Excuse me, may I please use your phone.

MARY
(sarcastically)
Bill, why don't you ask her... she's your
special friend...why is she wearing your
glasses.

An VOICE from upstairs answers.

MOTHER
Ain't got one.

MOTHER is standing at the bottom of the stairs. She is in her fifties, but looks younger. A sleazy, white trash queen.

DENISE
Huh? Oh, hi. You really don't have a
phone.

MOTHER
No, none. I had one once back in 57
maybe... I don't know. Really ain't
nobody we wanna be jaw flapping at around
here no more.

JERRY
Hey, maybe the guy with the towtruck
could drive us to a phone.

MOTHER
(she moves toward them)
His name is Rufus, Rufus Jr., but we all
call him RJ.

(CONTINUED)

52 CONTINUED: 52

JERRY
Oh, right.

MOTHER
What do they call you, sweety?

Mother shakes Jerry's hand, but doesn't let go.

JERRY
Um, I'm Jerry... that's Bill...Denise and Mary.

BILL
Yeah, maybe R.J. could just tow us and our car to the nearest garage.

DENISE
I mean obviously we will compensate you for your troubles.

MOTHER
Oh, you ain't no troubles, no, no, no fuss.
(claps her hands)
Baby... go see what Rufus Jr. is doing with these nice folks automobile.

BABY
(whining)
But, I'm watching something.

MOTHER
Baby, now git.

Baby sticks out her tongue, then slowly rises like a defiant child and walks out of the room.

MOTHER (CONT'D)
In the meanwhile please make yourselves at home.

DISSOLVE TO :

MONTAGE 53

Gruesome crime scene photos flash across the screen.

CHILDREN
(singing, off screen)
98 bodies in your bed,
Some are green, some are red.
Eat the flesh and pick the bones,
Drink the blood when you get home.
(MORE)

(CONTINUED)

HOUSE OF
1000 CORPSES

53 CONTINUED: 53

CHILDREN (cont'd)
99 bodies in the ground,
Some are blue, some are brown.
Gather round the people said,
Where do you go when you are dead?

54 INT. FARMHOUSE - LIVING ROOM - NIGHT 54

Mother, Jerry, Denise and Mary are all seated on the sofa. Bill sits in an easy chair.

MOTHER
So, what brings you kids way out here, ain't you got something better to do for Halloween than wander around out here in the sticks?

JERRY
Well. I thought I'd maybe take in a hoedown.

MOTHER
(flirting)
Oh, really...
(puts her hand on Jerry's knee and winks)
... well, I'm a pretty good dancer if you know what I mean... I bet I got a few moves you ain't never seen.

JERRY
I don't doubt that.

DENISE
No, he's just joking. We don't really have any plans other than spending the night at my Dad's house...
(glances at Jerry)
...which is where we were headed when our car broke down.

MOTHER
That's nice.

DENISE
Yeah, I guess I'll just help him hand out candy to the trick or treaters.

JERRY
And I'm gonna help put the razor blades in the candy apples.

MOTHER
I'll bet you are... you are a naughty little thing aren't ya.

(CONTINUED)

54 CONTINUED: 54

JERRY
I was just kidding.

Bill and Mary snicker at Jerry's comments. Denise tries to keep a straight face.

MOTHER
Oh, I get it... I guess you think your too good for the simple pleasures of Halloween.

MARY
No, just a little too old.

MOTHER
Oh really, well I hope something changes your mind someday.

Baby returns from the garage.

note: Intercut with T.V. possibly move change

BABY
Tiny's home.

MOTHER
What about R.J.?

BABY
Oh, he was already gone before I seen him... but Tiny saw him and said he said he was going out to the yard to get a new wheel.

BILL
The yard what's that?

MOTHER
It's an old auto junkyard out in Baldwin.

DENISE
How long is that gonna take?

MOTHER
He should be back in a couple hours.

MARY
A couple hours!

DENISE
Can't Tiny drive us to a phone.

Mother and Baby laugh.

Rob - Always nice But always seen when a genius is also so damn cute! Best to you in all your endeavors!

54 CONTINUED:

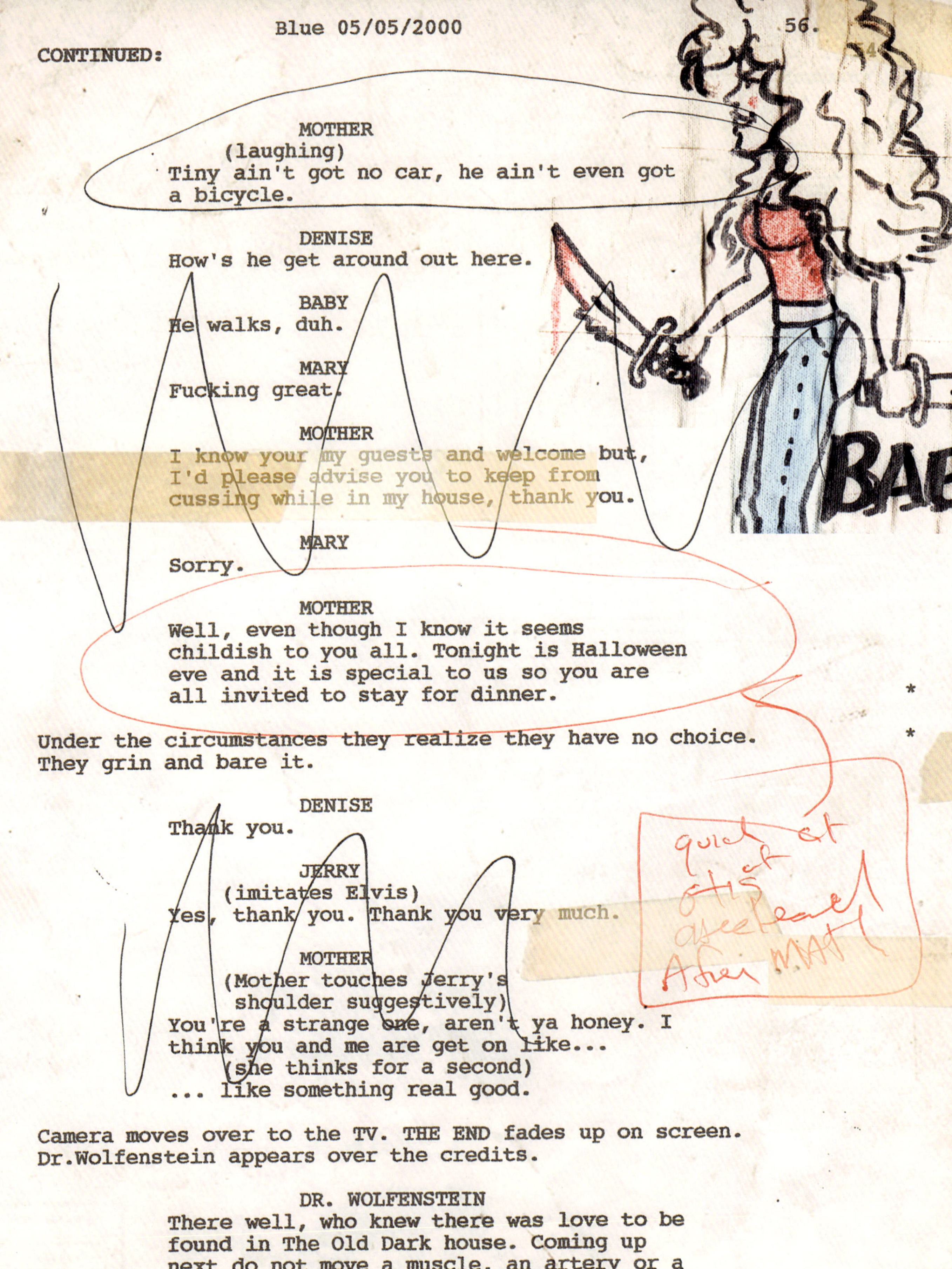

MOTHER
(laughing)
Tiny ain't got no car, he ain't even got a bicycle.

DENISE
How's he get around out here.

BABY
He walks, duh.

MARY
Fucking great.

MOTHER
I know your my guests and welcome but, I'd please advise you to keep from cussing while in my house, thank you.

MARY
Sorry.

MOTHER
Well, even though I know it seems childish to you all. Tonight is Halloween eve and it is special to us so you are all invited to stay for dinner. *

Under the circumstances they realize they have no choice. They grin and bare it. *

DENISE
Thank you.

JERRY
(imitates Elvis)
Yes, thank you. Thank you very much.

MOTHER
(Mother touches Jerry's shoulder suggestively)
You're a strange one, aren't ya honey. I think you and me are get on like...
(she thinks for a second)
... like something real good.

Camera moves over to the TV. THE END fades up on screen. Dr.Wolfenstein appears over the credits.

DR. WOLFENSTEIN
There well, who knew there was love to be found in The Old Dark house. Coming up next do not move a muscle, an artery or a
(MORE)

(CONTINUED)

Hartman

54 CONTINUED: 54

DR. WOLFENSTEIN (cont'd)
vein as we venture into another creepy classic... are you ready for The WOLFMAN, baby.

55 INT. HOUSE - DINNING ROOM 55

Bill, Jerry, Mary and Denise are now all seated around a large dinning room table. A thick mountain of candles sits burning dead center on the table giving off a warm glow. Dozens of Halloween decorations dangle from strings over the table, spiders, bats and black cats.

There is a hand-made PAPER MACHE MASK sitting on each plate.

MARY
(holding up the witch mask)
I hope to Christ she don't expect us to wear these things.

BILL
What ever it is just do. The more we play along the faster we'll get the hell out of here.

DENISE
Really, now is not the time to make waves.

JERRY
(pointing to a huge wooden chair) *
Dig that crazy chair, that must be reserved for Lurch. *

DENISE
Shhhhhh.

Mother walks in holding a covered serving tray.

DENISE (CONT'D)
You sure you don't need any help in there?

MOTHER
No dear, I'm fine. Now, what kind of host would I be if I put my guests to this kind of work.

She sets the tray and goes back in the kitchen.

BOOM! The sound of the front door SLAMMING shut is heard, followed by the POUNDING of heavy footsteps.

Mother's and Baby's shouting is heard.

(CONTINUED)

55 CONTINUED: 55

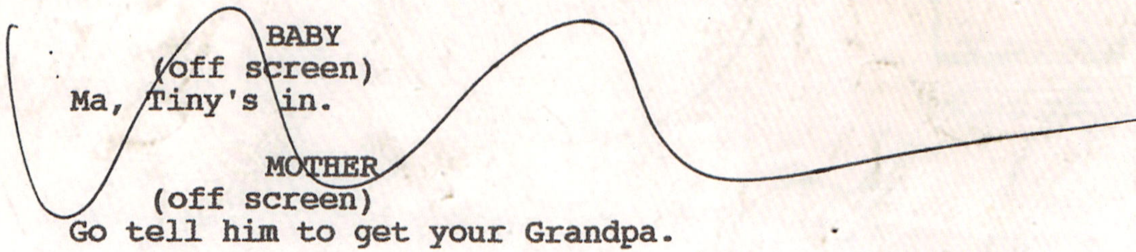

BABY
(off screen)
Ma, Tiny's in.

MOTHER
(off screen)
Go tell him to get your Grandpa.

56 INT. HOUSE - BABY'S ROOM 56

Baby is standing in front of her closet staring at her clothes. The walls of her room are covered with B+W photos of movie stars.

BABY
(whining)
Ma, I can't I'm busy getting dressed.

57 INT. HOUSE - DINING ROOM 57

TINY ENTERS and removes his coat.

Everyone is speechless.

Tiny is over SEVEN FEET TALL and weights THREE HUNDRED POUNDS. He is wearing a black sweater with a big red skull stitched into it. A red leather space mask covers his face. Black gloves cover his hands. *

Tiny sits at the table, looks down at his plate and says nothing.

Mother comes to fetch Tiny, she relays a message to him by writing on a small notebook, she holds it in front of his eyes. * * *

Tiny gets up and leaves the room.

MOTHER
You'll have to forgive Tiny, he can't hear so much.

DENISE
Oh.

MOTHER
Yeah, my poor baby. It's his Daddy's fault. I mean Earl was a good man... I mean he never hit me or nothing, but one day he just got up and went pure devil on us all.

(CONTINUED)

younger
brother. huge
and deformed.
mask covers
face of bones
childlike
personality
A playful
doesn't know
right from wrong
CHEAP

57 CONTINUED: 57

DENISE
What happened? Oh, I'm sorry it's none of my business.

MOTHER
He tried to burn the house down, said it was possessed by the spirits. Tiny was sleeping in the basement where the fire started. I don't think Earl ever meant to harm us... but Tiny was badly burnt, his ears were destroyed and most of his skin.

BILL
Is that why he wears the mask?

MOTHER
Yeah, my baby boy gets shy around new people, but he'll warm up to ya... especially the ladies.

JERRY
Great. I thought I felt a certain attraction between Mary and Tiny soon as he walked in.

MOTHER
Maybe. He's a real lady killer.

JERRY
Didn't ya think, Mary?

Mary just smiles, then gives Jerry a dirty look.

MOTHER
Well, we'll see... the night is young and so are you... o'well couple more minutes.

Mother returns to the kitchen.

DENISE
(elbows Jerry)
Don't be such a fucking smart ass.

MARY
Yeah, it's really your fault that we're stuck in this shithole in the first place.

JERRY
Oh, don't worry she didn't get offended by what I said. You two got to lighten up... right, Bill?

(CONTINUED)

ZOMBIE

Rob
Thank you very much for a great opportunity & providing a wonderful crew of people with whom to work. Best of luck in all you do!
PANAVISION
CHEAP ASS
HALLOWEEN
COSTUME

New Scenes

BABY with Cheerleaders

BABY

You're gonna miss a good show Tonight, but that's your tough luck.

I thought you kids were all about team spirit.

I mean you ~~[illegible]~~ fuck or cheer we aint done up since you got here.

Gimme a B
Gimme an A
Gimme a B
Gimme a Y — what's that spell?
(screaming...)

BABY you damn right

57 CONTINUED:

BILL
Whatever, at this point all I care about is food. I'm starving and I got a fucking killer headache.

JERRY
Hey, I asked you if you wanted some chicken.

BILL
Didn't look like chicken to me, more like fried pussy cat.

JERRY
(shrugs)
Tasted pretty good.

58 INT. FARMHOUSE - GRAMPA'S ROOM - NIGHT 58

In a cramped, darken room we see the huge shape of Tiny hovering over a BED containing the hunched, fragile old body of GRAMPA.

Grampa struggles to sit, then slowly slides his legs over the edge of the bed. Tiny helps him to stand.

GRAMPA
God Damn it, I can do it. I can do it, myself ya big monkey. I ain't dead yet... so don't you and your sister start counting out my money yet.

Grampa steadies himself against Tiny. They slowly walk out of the room.

GRAMPA (CONT'D)
God damn, my dogs are barking.

As they move into the light of the hallway, it is clear that Grampa is in his late 80's.

move as INSERT

Grampa quickly grows tired. Tiny picks him up into his arms and carries him down the stairs to the dinning room.

As they move past, the camera comes to rest on a STRANGE OBJECT sitting on a shelf.

move to 61s

A LARGE GLASS JAR containing a DEFORMED BABY. The pickled punk looks to have a small second head growing from its temple. The label on the jar reads STUFFY 1973.

The sound from the TV fades up in the background. BELA LUGOSI'S VOICE can be heard.

(CONTINUED)

58 CONTINUED: 58

BELA LUGOSI
(V.O.)
Your hands please, your left hand shows your past...

DISSOLVE TO :

59 TV SCREEN 59

Bela is seen as fortune teller holding a woman's hands. This is a scene from The Wolfman.

check clearance report

BELA LUGOSI
(CONT'D)
...and your right hand shows your future.

CLOSE UP

We see a tight shot of the woman's palm. A pentagram appears.

INT. DENISE'S FATHER HOUSE - NIGHT

We PULL BACK from the TV to find a Donald Willis sitting in a old easy chair. The room is modest, but comfortable.

He reaches over and picks up a small alarm clock, notices the time, concerned look comes over his face.

The phone rings. He quickly answers it.

MR.WILLIS
Hello, Denise.

Disappointment. He mutes the TV.

MR.WILLIS (CONT'D)
Oh, yeah...no, Fred. I was hoping you were Denise, she's a little late.
(pausing)
Yeah, yeah I'm sure the rain just slowed'em down....yeah...uh-huh, yeah... no, no you can keep it 'til Tuesday... alright talk to ya tomorrow, bye.

Unmutes the sound on the TV.

60 INT. DINNING ROOM - NIGHT 60

The feast is on. Mother, Tiny, Grampa, Jerry, Bill, Mary and Denise are gathered around the table.

60 CONTINUED: 60

MOTHER
Ok everyone, put on your masks. We can't very well eat with our everyday faces exposed.

Mother puts on her mask, Tiny and Grampa follow. Jerry, Bill and Denise slowly raise up their masks, Mary hesitates.

GRAMPA
(to Mary)
Christ kid, put it on. She ain't letting any of us touch the grub 'til your wearing the damn thing.

Mary rolls her eyes and complies.

JERRY
I've been meaning to ask you Mrs... Firefly
Ummmm.

MOTHER
(hesitates)
Firefly.

JERRY
Firefly... mmmmm odd name. Mrs. Firefly, do you know anything about the legend of Dr. Satan.

BILL
He we go.

Grampa shifts his eyes onto Mother.

MOTHER
(nervously)
Well, I'm not much for local gossip an this and that, but I've heard it mentioned in passing over the years but... I mean folks is queer and they say things, crazy things you know what I mean?

Otis Enters

GRAMPA
It's all talk, yakty yak, like a bunch of hungry chipmunks...Christ, Dr. Satan that takes the bull's nuts alright...
(starts laughing)
... hey, I hear some genius up north got a hot line on the Easter Bunny for ya.

A voice from the shadows interrupts.

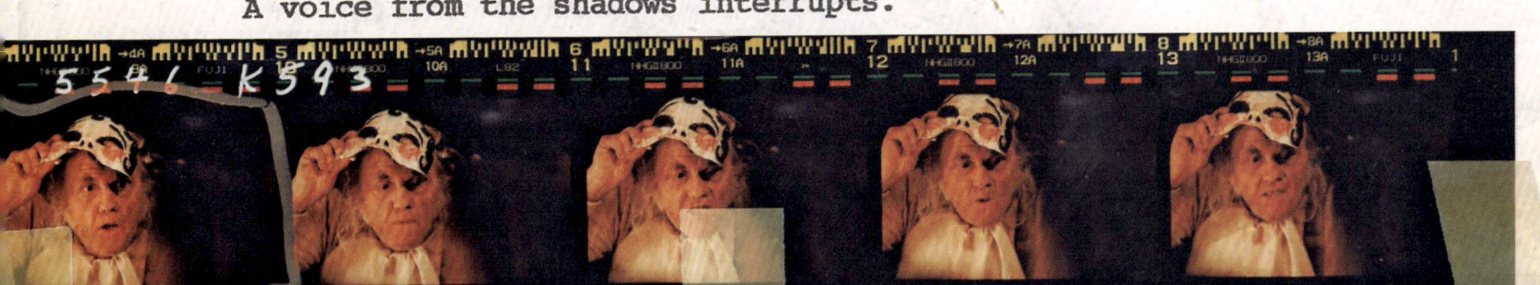

5546 K614
8 →8A 9 →9A 10 →10A 11 →11A 12
14 NHGII800 14A 15 NHGII800 15A 16 NHGII800 16A 17

OTIS
(slowly)
I know all about what you want to know all about.

A PALE FIGURE creeps forward like NOSFERATU from a dark corner of the room. This is OTIS.

He stands six foot, but is deathly slim. His skin is translucent, glowing in the dark. Long thin white hair covers his head. His eyes are grey. He is an ALBINO.

He is holding GLASS JAR containing a SMALL FETUS. On closer inspection we see there are two small bodies joined to one head. The label reads WOLF.

MOTHER
(happy surprise)
Otis! I can't believe you decided to come down and join us... and you brought little Wolf. This really is a special night... all my babies together.

Otis sets the disturbing jar of Wolf on the table. He leans forward onto the jar, resting is chin.

OTIS
Now, I don't know where you heard all your little fairy fables about Dr.Satan but...

BILL
From a Captain Spaulding down at some museum.

OTIS
(laughing)
That old bitch hog don't know shit. He tells cute little tattle-tales to sell his junk, but he don't sell no Yankee boys, no truth.

JERRY
But something happened right? I mean the story is based on a real incident, right?

GRAMPA
(mouth full of food)
What are you Jimmy Olsen cub reporter for the Daily Asshole.

MOTHER
Grampa... watch the language.

BURN THIS FLAG
BURN THIS FLAG
Otis
Driftwood
ZOMBIE
The boogie man is
real, AND you
found him!
Thanks for taking
a chance on me.
Bill Moseley

60 CONTINUED: 60

OTIS
I ain't sure that you really need to know. It's better you go home still dreaming about your kitty cats and puppy dogs.

JERRY
I really want to know.

GRAMPA
Hey, the kid wants to know. Enlighten him.

OTIS
Boy, I bet you'd stick your head in the fire, if I told ya you'd see hell... meanwhile you too stupid to realize you got a demon sticking out your ass singing," Holy Miss Moly, I got a live one.".

DENISE
Can we please change the subject.

The CLOCK on the wall strikes TEN.

GRAMPA
(shouting)
Dinner's over.
(pushes his plate back and stands up)
Ladies and Germs... it's showtime.

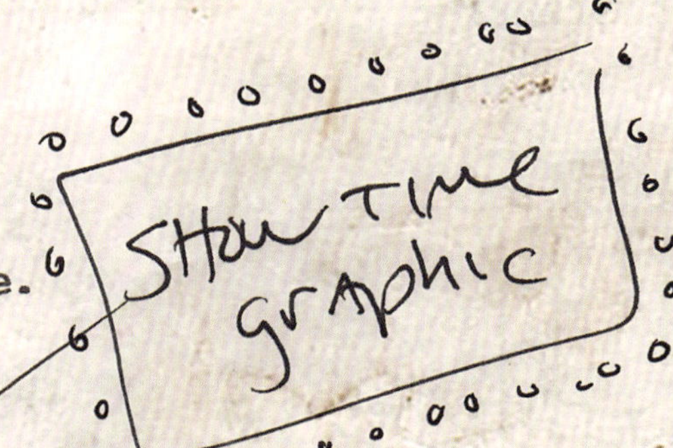

Grampa hobbles out of the room.

BILL
What's he so excited about?

DENISE
Yeah, showtime for what?

MOTHER
For the show. It's Halloween eve and time for our show.

JERRY
Oh, you mean on TV.

MOTHER
No, no, no it's so much more special than that... you'll see, you'll be the first to ever see. I think this is something you'll really love.

60 CONTINUED: 60

JERRY
Great.

A60 EXT. FARMHOUSE - BARN - NIGHT A60

Bill, Jerry, Mary and Denise stand waiting in front of a old barn. Tiny unlocks the doors huge doors of the barn and swings them open.

Stand inside waiting is Mother. She is all dressed up for the occasion.

MOTHER
Please, come in... how many in your party...
(she counts the heads)
... one, two, three and four... right this way.

Mother hands each of them a folded piece of paper, which serves as a program book. Hand draw on each is a orange pumpkin.

61 INT. FARMHOUSE - BARN - NIGHT 61

We follow Mother inside.

Thousand of red Christmas lights hang down, strung through the rotting wood rafters. Crates, barrels and an odd assortment of chairs face a large quilted curtain. Filling these seats are LIFELESS DUMMIES.

MOTHER
Please be seated.

Mother motions toward four empty seats in the front row.

JERRY
(whispering)
This is way too fucked up for words.

MARY
(loud whisper)
I know the words...fucking psycho fucking bullshit, that's the words.

BILL
Just grin and bear it.

DENISE
That food...
(holding stomach)
ugh, I feel like I'm gonna puke.

(CONTINUED)

WHY?

NO TURNING BACK!
HOUSE OF 1000 CORPSES

61 CONTINUED: 61

Jerry, Bill, Mary and Denise take their seats.

Mary flips open the program. Inside, written in crayon, are the words: HALLOWEEN EXTRAVAGANZA - starring the Comedy Legend GRAMPA and the World Famous BABY.

MARY
(to Bill)
Check this out.

BILL
Well, ya can't complain I never take you anyplace.

The sound of a warped crackling record fills the room. Lounge music.

A small spotlight hits the quilted curtain covering the stage. Mother Firefly stands behind the controls. She is smiling proudly.

The curtain clumsily parts TO REVEAL :

A stage set pieced together from amusement park wreckage. A giant painted plywood devil looms over the stage, surrounded by dancing skeletons and demons girls.

A microphone stands center stage.

note: Split Screens

BILL (CONT'D)
(quietly)
I can't believe what I'm seeing.

JERRY
I know this is fucking nuts.

MARY
This starting to make me real uncomfortable.

BILL
Just sit back and enjoy the show.

The sound of CANNED APPLAUSE fills the room. Bill begins to applaud, Jerry and Denise join in. Mary does not.

GRAMPA
(v.o.)
Ladies and gentlemen, straight from his smash six week sold out run at Tiki-Ti Club... the Stardust lounge is proud to present Mr. Sexy himself... Grampa Hugo.

(CONTINUED)

A Talent Agency

DENNIS FIMPLE

SAG / AFTRA

Height: 5'8"
Weight: 150 lbs.

Hair: Grey / Brown
Eyes: Blue

SEE
TONIGHT ONLY
HARE-LIP
3 BALLS $1
STRANGE BUT TRUE!

Rob-
THANK you for the
space to create -
Dennis
Pimple
"The DR."

61 CONTINUED: 61

Grampa walks out to center stage, mic in hand and begins to speak.

GRAMPA (CONT'D)
Hey, let me tell ya a story... so I'm hanging out with my buddy Hal Jackowictz and I'm like hey Hal, lets go get some booze and chase the chickens... fucking Hal says no, no the old battle axe at home will break my balls... I gotta get my ass home.

The kids stare in shock at Grampa. Jerry begins to laugh.

GRAMPA (CONT'D)
(cont'd)
So, I tell'em... Hal here's the secret. Go home tonight crawl into bed, get under the covers and eat your wife's pussy...I mean jam your face right in the bush.

Jerry starts to giggle.

DENISE
(quietly)
What are you laughing at?

JERRY
I don't know I think he's funny.

DENISE
This isn't funny, its twisted.

GRAMPA
So, Hal goes home jumps in starts chomping and licking away at her pussy, she's screaming and howling... she totally passes out from the experience.

MARY
Dear God, let this end.

GRAMPA
Now, Hal... He's feeling pretty good, so he goes into the bathroom for a quick shave...
(pauses)
...suddenly, he lets out a horrible scream. Ahhhhhhhhhhhhhh!

The recorded crowd chuckles.

(CONTINUED)

more shadows around eyes;
no Beard, long sideburns / needs to be more realistic
too Humorous — not scary
TOBOR

61 CONTINUED: 61

GRAMPA (CONT'D)
Sitting there on the toilet is Hal's wife Gloria... and she says, "Quiet down, you'll wake Grandma!"

The recorded crowd screams with laughter, as does Jerry. Bill, Denise and Mary look at him like he's crazy.

GRAMPA (CONT'D)
Thank you your too kind, too kind... stay in your seats coming up next we got something special for you men out there.

The curtains close and the stage goes dark.

next attraction graphic

DENISE
Shit, I'm all for being a sport but, this is ridiculous.

BILL
(looking at his watch)
Man, it's already ten thirty.

MARY
I'm with Denise, can't we just walk to someplace, this is getting fucking stupid.

JERRY
Negative. Shit, we are so deep in the sticks we could walk for hours and find zero.

BILL
Yeah, I'd say at this point all we can do just wait it out. There's nothing else.

DENISE
I suppose, I mean they're obviously all bonkers, but I guess their harmless.

MARY
I fucking hope so.

Song: Helen Kane

The stage lights come up. The recorded applause and music begin.

Baby enters the stage. She is dressed in a home-made showgirl outfit. She begins to dance clumsily to the music. She appears to be somewhat intoxicated.

The vocals come on and Baby begins to lipsync to the song.

(CONTINUED)

36A
36
32

DENISE
You gotta be kidding me. This chick is wasted.

JERRY
Shhhhhh.

MARY
How much is a person suppose to stand?

BILL
(motioning for Mary to keep her voice down)
Quiet.

MARY
(sarcastically)
Oh, I'm sorry bothering you? Was I disturbing your viewing pleasure.

Baby makes her way down from the stage on to floor level. She gyrates and seductively TEASES one of the dummy audience members.

Baby moves over to Jerry. Stroking her hand down his face. Denise tries to look amused. Jerry smiles uncomfortably.

Baby strolls past Denise and stops in front of Mary. Baby pauses and pinches Mary's cheek and winks. Mary is FURIOUS.

Baby moves over to Bill. Mary watches like a mother hawk. Baby sings and dances with all of her attention focused on Bill.

Baby puts her arms around Bill's neck and sits on his lap. Mary BOLTS FORWARD and SHOVES Baby off of Bill. Baby crashes onto the floor.

MARY (CONT'D)
Take that you fucking slut!
(Mary spits at Baby)
Fucking redneck whore!

BABY
You shouldn't a done that.

MARY
Why? You gonna do something about?

BABY
(standing up)
Yeah, I'll do something motherfucker.

Track from behind

5546 THE HOUSE OF 1000 CORPSES

61 CONTINUED: 61

Baby takes out a straight razor from behind her back.

BABY (CONT'D) *
I'll cut your fucking tits off and shove down your throat.

MOTHER
Baby! Stop!

Mrs. Firefly runs down, from her position behind the spotlight, and intercedes.

BABY
Come on, ma... this bitch's got it coming.

MOTHER
No, I told you....

SCREECH! The garage door slides open. Rufus has returned.

RUFUS JR.
(interrupting)
Car's done.

DENISE
Thank God.

MOTHER
I suggest you kids leave now.

MARY
Don't worry I'm gone.

62 EXT. FARMHOUSE - NIGHT 62

Bill, Jerry, Denise and Mary climb back into their car.

BILL
Don't look back just get

DENISE
Lock the fucking doors.

MARY
Hurry up!

INT. CAR - NIGHT 63

Bill begins to pull the car down the long dirt driveway towards the road. The heavy rain makes visibility difficult.

BAD

63 CONTINUED: 63

BILL
(straining to see through the darkness)
Almost there.

JERRY
Jesus, you think she was really gonna cut you.

Mary looks out the window, watching the house as they pull away.

MARY
(leaning her forehead on the window)
Of course she was gonna cut me, she's a fucking nut...
(closes her eyes and take a breath)
I knew she was crazy from the second we picked her up.

SLAM! Suddenly, Baby pounds her fist against the Mary's window. Mary jumps back in terror.

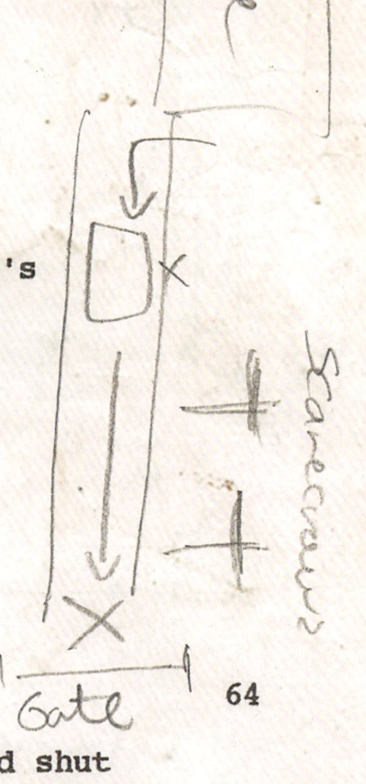

BABY
(screaming)
Your in Hell, bitch! Your gonna die like a dog!

Baby disappears into the darkness.

MARY
Go! Go! Go! Get us out of here!

64 EXT. FARMHOUSE - NIGHT 64

Bill pulls the car up to the front gate. It is chained shut with a huge padlock..

LIGHTNING CRASHES, illuminating the crucified scarecrows.

FLASH CLOSE-UP CUTS -

of grinning jack-o'-lantern faces peer down from above.

65 INT. CAR - NIGHT

Bill opens the car door, starts to get out.

MARY
(hysterical)
What are you doing!

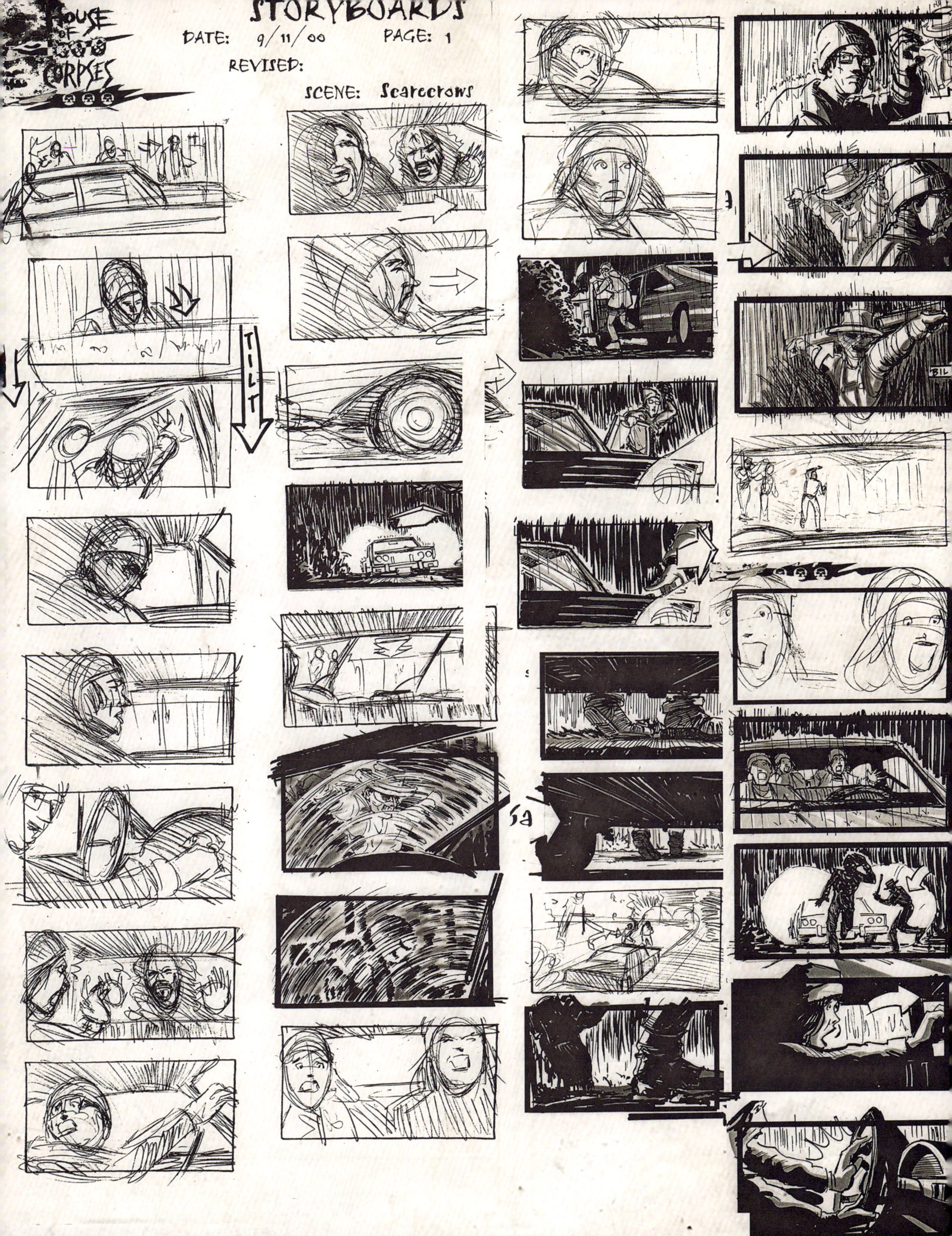

HOUSE OF 1000 CORPSES
STORYBOARDS
DATE: 9/11/00
PAGE: 1
REVISED:
SCENE: Scarecrows
TILT

65 CONTINUED: 65

BILL
I gotta open the gate.

MARY
Drive through it !

BILL
It won't work.

JERRY
Holy shit, hurry up!

Jerry, Mary and Denise watch through the windshield as Bill struggles to unlatch the thick iron gates.

SUDDENLY, one of the SCARECROWS JUMPS down from his cross and SMASHES Bill over the head with a HEAVY CLUB. Bill drops to his knees.

MARY
Bill! Help him!

Jerry throws opens his door to get out. He's SHOVED BACK into the car by another larger scarecrow outside his door. This scarecrow begins smashing the car's windows with a METAL PIPE.

Bill lays motionless face down in the mud. His attacker turns his attention on the car. He also begins smashing the car's windows.

Jerry goes to help
TINY SMASHES him into windshield

66 EXT. CAR - NIGHT 66

From a distance, we see Jerry pulled from the car and beaten. The girls are helplessly trapped inside the destroyed vehicle. The scarecrows continue to pound on the car.

As we fade out, the sound of a BARKING DOG can be heard.

FADE TO :

67 EXT. FARMHOUSE - MAGIC 67

From a long shot, we see the farmhouse in the early morning sunrise. All is still.

The sound of an engine starting breaks the eerie early morning silence. Rufus's tow truck is seen pulling away from behind the house. The BEATEN REMAINS of Bill's car are towed behind it.

Otis remove mask
Tiny breaks window to drag out Denise
Otis smashes windshield with pipe - climbs on car and screams in rain.

HONK!
HONK!
15
WHIP
15a
WHIP
TINY
19

8
8A
9
9A
10
10A
13
KODAK PORTRA 800
14
KODAK PORTRA 800
15
KODAK POR
5546 K2364

THUD!
MASK
28
8a
THUD!
THUD!
PAN
PAN

A67 EXT. WILLIS HOUSE - SUNRISE A67

All is calm on this quiet suburban street.

68 INT. WILLIS HOUSE - SUNRISE 68

Darkness, except for the face of an alarm clock. The time is 7:00 AM. TICK, TICK, TICK... BUZZZZZZ. The alarm goes off.

A hand reaches over and turns off the alarm. We hear a deep groan. A light turns on.

INT. WILLIS'S LIVING ROOM - MORNING

Don Willis wakes up, having fallen asleep in his easy chair. He sits up and wipes the sleep from his eyes. He runs a hand across his head, smoothing out his thinning grey hair.

He picks up the phone, dials a number, waits.

MR.WILLIS

Hi. Lieutenant Brockman. please... Donald Willis.

He holds.

MR.WILLIS (CONT'D)

Hey, Phil...

(listens)

Yeah, I'm alright...but I need you to check on something for me.

Willis stands, walks to the window, opens the shades, morning sun fills the room.

A shelf by the window is cluttered with framed photographs. B+W memories of Denise at the beach, RUDY the dog, High School graduations and Donald Willis in uniform with the other members of 56 Precinct. Donald is an FORMER POLICE OFFICER.

MR.WILLIS (CONT'D)

I'm a little worried about Denise. She called me last night from the road, out by Ruggsville at some joint called Spaulding's or something like that, said she'd be here about eleven... but she never show up.

(CONTINUED)

DUNCE
Hartman

CONTINUED:

MR.WILLIS (CONT'D)
Yeah, if you could run a check on up that way and see about any accidents or road closing or anything, I'd really appreciate it...
(listening)
...yeah, yeah, I know... I'm sure nothing happened but, you know me I like to worry.... thanks...bye.

Hangs up the phone.

69 INT. FARMHOUSE - OTIS'S ROOM - DAY 69

Mary opens her eyes, squinting into the light. Sunlight peers through filth of the windows, fractured by the tattered remains of rotted curtains. Peeling yellowed newspaper serves as wallpaper surrounding the window.

Mary's eyes move across the walls to a painting of a BIG EYED KITTEN. She stares at it and smiles. A look a horror begins to appear on her face. She begins to scream uncontrollably

OTIS
(off screen)
Shut your fucking mouth!

She is hysterical.

OTIS (CONT'D)
I said shut your mouth!

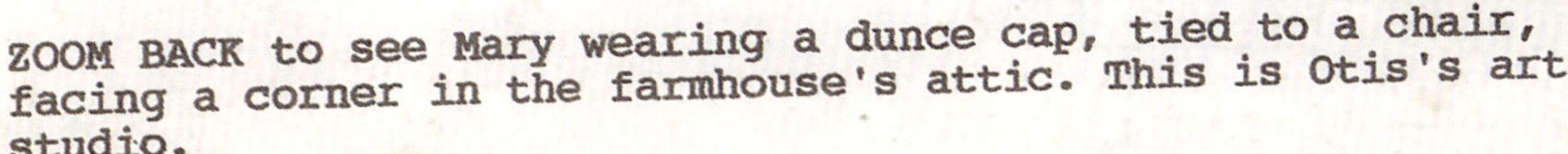

ZOOM BACK to see Mary wearing a dunce cap, tied to a chair, facing a corner in the farmhouse's attic. This is Otis's art studio.

Otis, standing before a large canvas, sets down his paint brush and calmly walks over to Mary.

He spins her chair around, clamps her mouth shut with his hand and leans his nose against hers.

OTIS (CONT'D)
(slow and sinister)
Listen, you Malibu Barbie middle class piece of shit. I'm trying to work, you got me, work...you ever work?

Mary eyes scream with terror, she nods yes.

OTIS (CONT'D)
Yeah, I'll bet you did. Scooping ice cream to your shitheel friends on summer
(MORE)

(CONTINUED)

全米ベスト10入り！上映禁止ギリギリ超過激作が遂に解禁！！
FUN FOR ALL!!
JOURNEY INTO DANGER?
1000の恐怖が眠る館へようこそ。
ロブ・ゾンビ監督作品
マーダー・ライド・ショー
RED HOT PUSSY LIQUORS
LIONS GATE FILMS PRESENTS A ROB ZOMBIE FILM HOUSE OF 1000 CORPSES STARRING SID HAIG BILL MOSELEY SHERI MOON AND KAREN BLACK
CASTING BY DONALD PAUL PEMRICK AND DEAN E. FRONK MUSIC BY ROB ZOMBIE AND SCOTT HUMPHREY COSTUME DESIGNS BY AMANDA FRIEDLAND
SPECIAL MAKE-UP EFFECTS BY WAYNE TOTH EDITED BY KATHRYN HIMOFF ROBERT K. LAMBERT, A.C.E. AND SEAN LAMBERT PRODUCTION DESIGN BY GREGG GIBBS
DIRECTOR OF PHOTOGRAPHY TOM RICHMOND AND ALEX POPPAS ASSOCIATE PRODUCER JOEL HATCH CO-PRODUCER DANIELLE SHILLING LOVETT
EXECUTIVE PRODUCER ANDREW D. GIVEN GUY OSEARY PRODUCED BY ANDY GOULD WRITTEN AND DIRECTED BY ROB ZOMBIE
LIONS GATE FILMS
GEFFEN
UMG SOUNDTRACKS
SDDS Sony Dynamic Digital Sound
dts
DOLBY SR
R-15
Art Port

69 CONTINUED: 69

OTIS (CONT'D)
break... well, I ain't talking about white socks with Mickey Mouse on one side and Donald Duck on the other... shit, you ain't reading no funny books, mamma.

Otis raises his paint covered hand.

OTIS (CONT'D)
This is blood and guts, Susy Q. Our bodies come and go, but this blood is forever...
(pulls a small book from his breast pocket)
... let me read you something, listen and learn... you listening?

Otis pulls back his hand, ready to backhand her across the face with the book. She nods again. He lowers the book.

OTIS (CONT'D)
(gesturing dramatically)
And the angels, all pallid and wan,
Uprising, unveiling, affirm
That the play is the tragedy "Man"
And its hero the Conqueror Worm
(pauses)
...you get that? Art is eternal, you get me, mamma?

too much

Mary stares dumbfounded.

OTIS (CONT'D)
Now, I'm gonna remove my hand... you make a sound and I swear I'll slit you open and make you eat your own fucking intestines... you get me?

She nods again. He slowly removes his hand from her mouth. Mary tries to remain calm, but starts to hyperventilate. Tears roll down her face.

Fish boy

MARY
(whispering)
Why? Why are you doing this?

OTIS
Doing what? Messy up your day? Well, fuck lady there are some bigger issues at hand... than your have a nice fucking day bumper sticker shit! *

MARY
Where's Bill?

(CONTINUED)

DUNCE
BURN THIS FLAG

69 CONTINUED: 69

OTIS
(chuckling)
Well, Bill... he's a good guy, he's been great help to me... a real blessing ...I could have asked for a better specimen. I mean you don't know what a dry spell I've had, total block...
(slaps his forehead)
...total block... but Bill he's OK.

Mary looks confused, but relieved.

MARY
(softly)
Where is he?

OTIS
Let's go see.

Otis grabs the back of the chair and drags her across the room towards a curtained off area.

Whoosh! He pulls her through the curtains. From behind the curtain we hear Mary SCREAMING and Otis LAUGHING.

MARY
(behind curtain)
Bill? No, no, no! What have you done, Bill!

70 INT. CURTAIN ROOM - OTIS'S ROOM - DAY 70

Ugliness. Decay. Pain. Carefully arranged on a model's platform is the severed torso of Bill sewn to a large homemade fish tail. He is lying on his right side posing.

Bill's face is frozen in death scream.

OTIS
Behold... The Fish-Boy!

MARY
(repeating to herself)
This can't be real, this can't be real, this can't be real.

OTIS
Oh, it's real... as real as I want it to be, mamma...
(grabs his canvas and holds it in her face)
...look, see the magic in my brush strokes.

70 CONTINUED: 70

Painted on the canvas is the gruesome scene of Bill as the Fish-Boy.

MARY
(crying)
Fuck you, you fucking freak!

OTIS
Oh, come now... were all creatures of God and freaks in our own way...
(twitches and shakes)
... but if you'll notice...
(points to a blank spot in the painting)
right here, needs a little something, heh?

Otis slowly puts down the canvas, turns and picks up a huge hunting knife.

MARY
What are you doing?
(squirming)
... no, stop... please, please.

OTIS
You, my dear little worm feeder are about to be come immortalized.

Otis draws back the knife.

MARY
(screaming)
Noooooooooooo!

Otis swings the knife forward, directly into the camera.

cut Hard to Ravelli Close up

A70 CLOSE UP - CLOWN FACE A70

Ravelli's clown head bobs back and forth.

PULL BACK to:

Ravelli, wearing his clown head, stands by the road side waving to passing cars.

71 EXT. SPAULDING'S - DAY 71

Music Cue — Buck Owens Who's gonna mow your grass

A police car drives pass Ravelli and comes to a stop. OFFICER GEORGE WYDELL, 42, a big, slightly paunchy man with a big mustache and mirrored sunglasses, steps from his car.

Call Tom Towles

(CONTINUED)

71 CONTINUED: 71

Following close behind, OFFICER STEVE NASH, 29, tall, athletic.

WYDELL
(pauses, looks around, pulls up his belt)
Well, let's go see if the nut that runs this place can help us.

NASH
I thought they sent us that old boy away on some kind of indecent exposure deal or something.

WYDELL
Naw, the charges never stuck.

They walk to the door.

72 INT. SPAULDING'S - DAY 72

The door swings open. Wydell enters slowly, putting on his best cowboy attitude. Nash follows suit.

Wydell, hands on his belt, struts up to the counter. No one is around.

A rusted belt sits on the counter, taped to it is a handwritten note, "ring for service". Wydell rings it once, waits, no response. Rings it again, waits, no response.

NASH
(looking around the room)
Get a load of all this crap... I'd red flag anybody running a joint like this.

Wydell begins ringing the bell non-stop.

Spaulding shouts from the backroom.

SPAULDING
Whoevers' a jerking off on that bell better be gone when I get out there... cause I'm gonna rip your nuts off.

Spaulding enters from behind the curtain, angry. He sees the troopers and puts on a phony grin.

SPAULDING (CONT'D)
Officers, officers what can I do for you today? I ain't fried up the birds yet... if that's what your ring a ding dinging about.

(CONTINUED)

BABY
HOUSE OF
1000 CORPSES

72 CONTINUED:

WYDELL
(pulls a paper from his pocket)
What I need from you are some answers about some missing kids..
(unfolds the paper to reveal a picture of Denise)

SPAULDING
Well, I'll try but I don't know nothing 'bout nobody. I'm a guy who likes to mine his own business, if ya get what I'm saying.

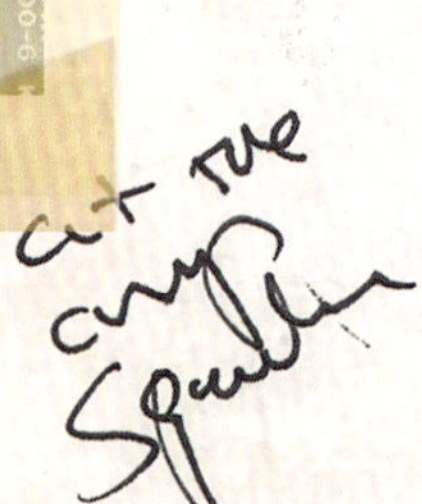

WYDELL
(holds up picture)
You seen this girl? Say... within the last 24 hours.

Spaulding reaches out and grabs the picture.

SPAULDING
(studies the picture)
Yeah, yeah I seen her. ~~Good look~~ cute ing kid, but not really my type...
(gesturing with his hands)
... I like meaty, eh?...the bigger the cushion, the sweeter the pushin', eh?

enters smoking

NASH
(losing patience)
Hey, ass clown how 'bout some answers. We ain't interested in your love life.

cut the crap Spaulding

WYDELL
~~Come on~~ Just, get with the facts.

SPAULDING
Hmmmmmmmmm?

WYDELL
What'd you see, who was she with, where were they going?

SPAULDING
Aw, she was with some nosey, smartass kids. They were pokin' around... asking stupid questions. *

NASH
Questions about what? *

Rob, if I could spell without a spell checker I would make this longer and more articulate and expensive. But since I don't, I'll just say I love you man, You Rock!!
Love Tom T.
"Wydell"

CHICKEN
GASOLINE
EXPERIENCE
REAL LIFE
HORROR
NOT FOR SISSIES
SEE THE MAN WITH 29 NEEDLES IN HIS GROIN
SEE THE PSYCHO OF PLAINFIELD A TRUE CANNIBAL
"House of 1000 Corpses"
Rob Zombie

HEY Rob...
Break A LEG!
AND EVERY OTHER
BODY PART...
Best wishes
"88" Keyes
RIFF

TOM TOWLES

Walton Goggins

5546 THE HOUSE OF 1000 CORPSES

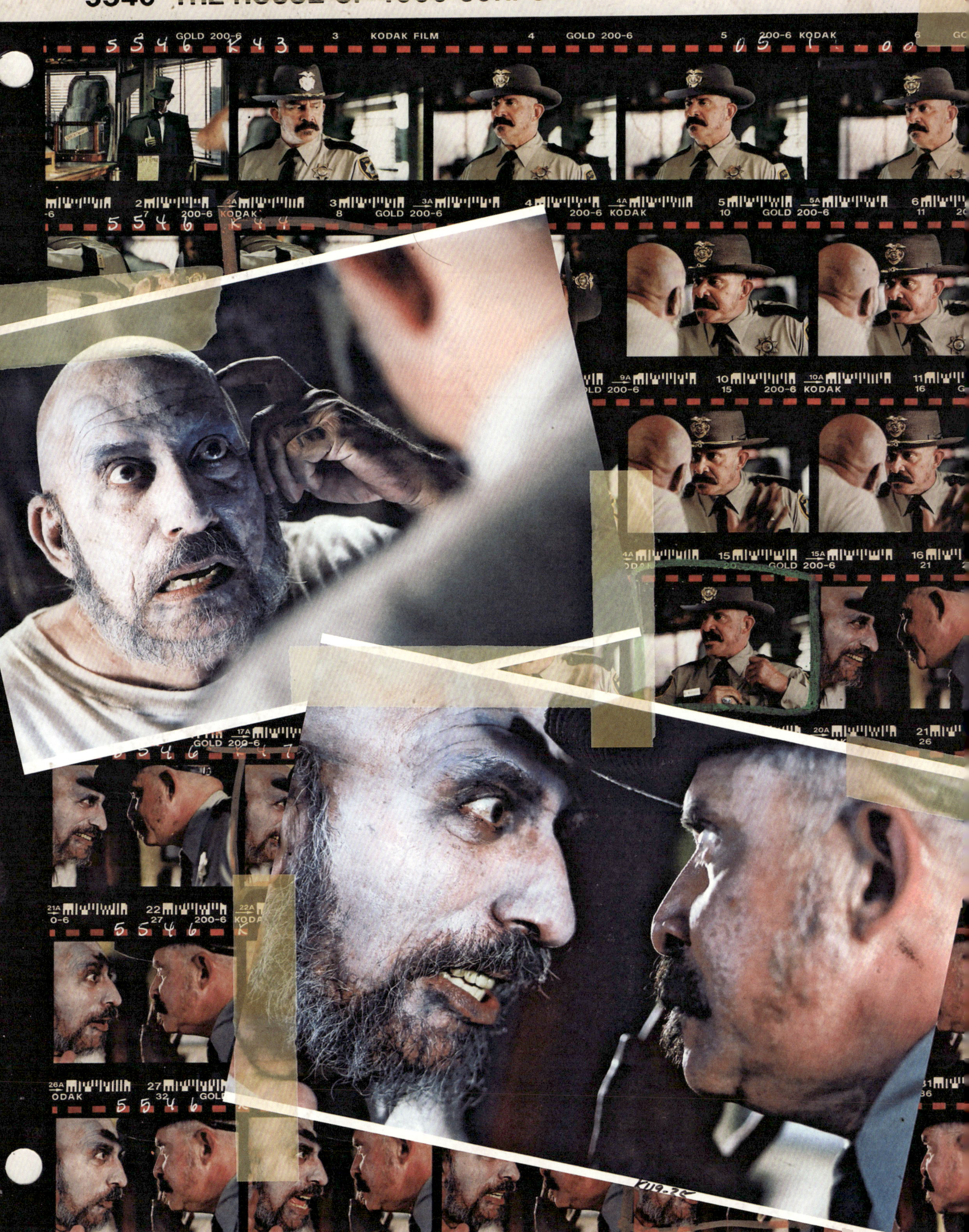

72 CONTINUED: 72

SPAULDING
This and that, mostly some tired Dr.Satan bullshit... they got a gander at the display back there and thought they could solve the great Deadwoods mystery.

WYDELL
And how they get that idea?

SPAULDING
Well, I gave'em direction out there, up by the old farm row... I figured what's the harm. It's good for my tourist trade, eh?

NASH
~~You can piss up a rope for all I care...what else?~~

SPAULDING
Nothing, stupid kids probably got themselves turned around backasswards and got lost.

WYDELL
Is that all... think real hard.

SPAULDING
Yeah, they weren't here but a few minutes, didn't really have time to get as up close and personal as I do with most of the assholes that wander through here.

WYDELL
How's about you give me those same directions.

SPAULDING
Yeah, yeah, sure. You don't have to get all True Grit all over my ass... I'll give'm to ya... you can knock yourself silly for all I care.

WYDELL
(hands him a note pad)
Enough talk, write.

73 OMIT 73

74 EXT. CHERRYPICKER RD.- WOODS - MIDDAY 74

The police cruiser maneuvers down the rough dirtroad.

MONSTERS
SEE
GAS 79¢
GAS 85¢
SEE THE HORROR
FUN FOR ALL AGES
Ravelli outside SPAULDINGS
Rehearsal @ 315P
Pick Up @ Hotel/
Rehearsal @ 8P
SW 10P Pick Up @ Home
Hold
SW 8P 10P Report to Location / Rehearsal @ 8P
SW 8P 10P
Hold
SWF 2P 4P Report to Location / Rehearsal @ 315P

75 INT. POLICE CAR - MIDDAY 75

Wydell and Nash scan the surrounding woods for any sign of Denise and her friends.

NASH
Boss, the way I see it is these kids probally stop off somewhere, bought a 12-pack of cold ones and are off getting shitfaced, knee deep in a piece of ass.

WYDELL
I hope you're right, but my guts are telling me different.

NASH
Your Spidey senses tingling.

WYDELL
Yeah...
(realizes what he just said)
... huh, what the hell are you talking about?

NASH
You know, your hyper sensitive spidey senses... like Spiderman...
(pauses)
...you know, like in the comics.

WYDELL
How old do you think I am? I know who the fuck Spiderman is. Get to your point.

NASH
You know his senses start tingling...when he was in approaching danger and shit.

WYDELL
I always favored the Hulk.

NASH
I always figured as much.

WYDELL
What is that supposed to mean...
(looking off to the side of the road)
...Aw, Christ.

NASH
What.

Review Godsell
Audition tapes

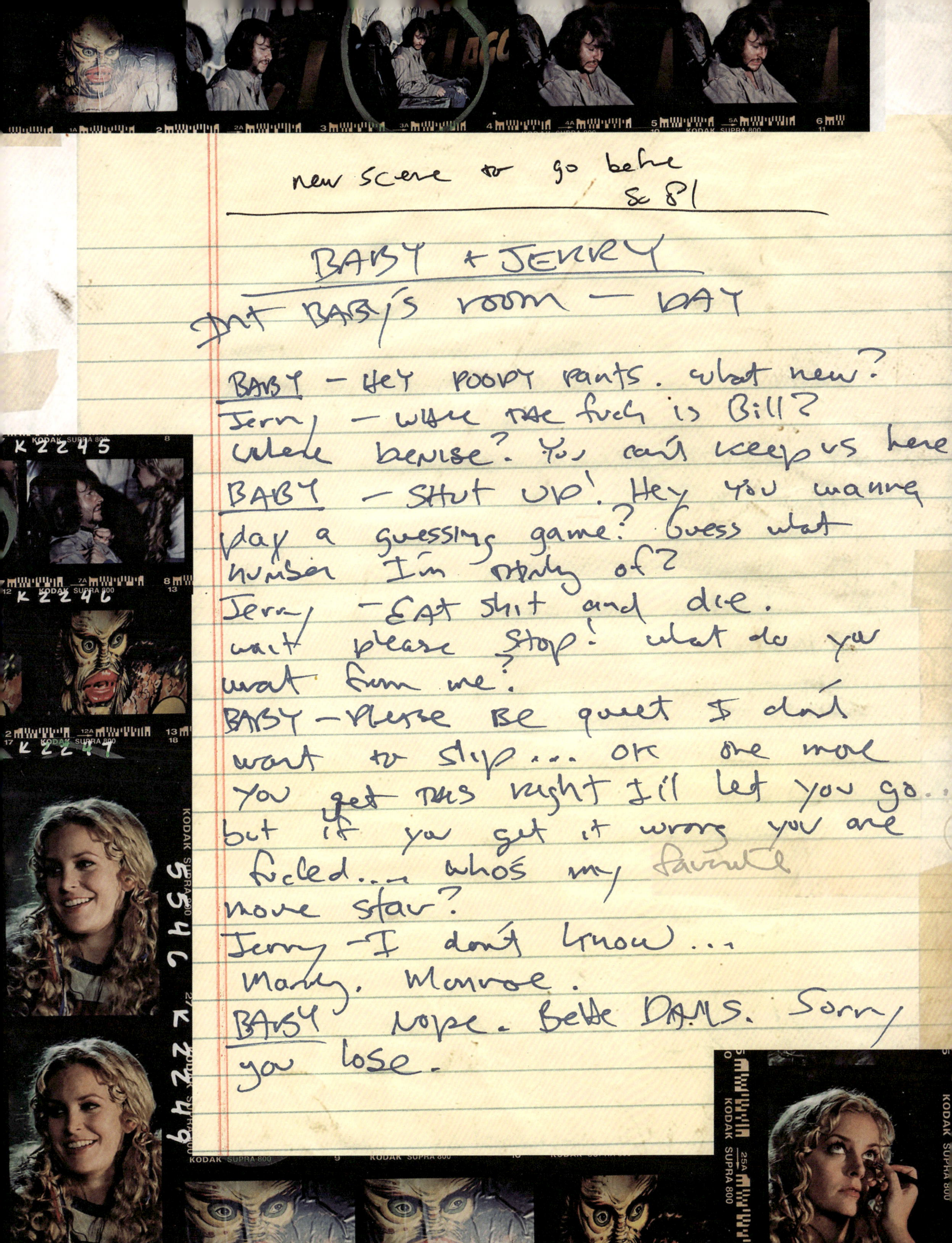

new scene to go before sc 81

BABY + JERRY

INT BABY's room — DAY

BABY — HEY POOPY pants. what new?
Jerry — where the fuck is Bill?
where Denise? You can't keep us here
BABY — SHUT UP! Hey You wanna
play a guessing game? Guess what
number I'm thinking of?
Jerry — EAT shit and die.
wait please stop! what do you
want from me?
BABY — please be quiet I don't
want to slip... ok one more
you get this right I'll let you go..
but if you get it wrong you are
fucked... who's my favorite
movie star?
Jerry — I don't know...
Marilyn. Monroe.
BABY Nope. Bette DAVIS. Sorry
you lose.

move Scene 81 here

76 ~~EXT.~~ CHERRYPICKER ROAD - WOODS - MIDDAY 76

Bill's car is down in a ditch, run off the side of the road.

77 INT. POLICE CAR - MIDDAY 77

Nash checks the license plate number with his sheet. *

NASH *
Plates match.

WYDELL
Call the chief... We found'em.

78-80 OMIT 78-80 *

new BABY + Jerry scene

81 EXT. CHERRYPICKER ROAD - WOODS - MIDDAY 81 *

Bill's car is now sitting in the middle of the road. The back is attached to a police towtruck. An additional police cruiser arrives on the scene.

Sheriff Huston steps out from his cruiser.

HUSTON
What'd we got ourselves here, George? *

WYDELL
A vehicle registered to a William S. Hudley.

HUSTON
Holy Jesus, somebody had themselves a field day beating the shit outta this thing.

WYDELL
Yeah, no mercy shown here.

HUSTON
~~Recover~~ didn't find any bodies? did ya?

WYDELL
Not yet.

HUSTON
(inspecting the car)
Shit, I wonder what these kids could have possibly done to bring this much hell down on 'em.

SHERIFF
THE INQUIZITOR

81 CONTINUED: 81

WYDELL
Just in the wrong place at the wrong time.

HUSTON
That the understatement of the year.

WYDELL
Yep, I suppose it is.

82 INT. BILL'S CAR - WOODS - MIDDAY 82

Nash is digging around under the front seat. *

NASH
Hey, I found something. *

Nash crawls out of the car.

83 EXT. CHERRYPICKER ROAD - WOODS -MIDDAY

HUSTON
What'd ya got there?

NASH
Keys...
(looks at the key chain)
...this is them, says Bill loves Mary right on the keychain.

HUSTON
Well Christ boy, don't stand there dog dicking around.

some prize dog dick open the trunk

crane up from the trunk to reveal scene

NASH
Huh?

HUSTON
Open up the trunk.

NASH
Yes, sir.

WYDELL
Toss'em over here.

Nash tosses them over the car to Wydell. Wydell fishes through the keys, finds the trunk key and opens it.

HUSTON
(winces and steps back)
God damn.

83 CONTINUED: 83

NASH
You find something, Georgie?

WYDELL
(disgusted)
Yep, I found something.

We move around the car to see the nude body of Karen Murphy laying in the trunk. Her arms and legs are hog tied. She is dead. The word TRICK is carved into her side.

A83 INT TOWTRUCK - DAY A83

We are cruising down the road. A bobbing head skeleton toy glued to the dashboard wiggles with each bump in the road. Behind the wheel is Rufus Jr., riding shotgun is Baby, dressed in her Sunday best. The radio is blasting.

BABY
(screaming over the music)
We're gonna have fun tonight, bro.

RUFUS JR.
Yeah, fun.

They speed off.

84 INT. FARMHOUSE BASEMENT- TINY'S ROOM - LATE AFTERNOON 84

Water drips down from the leaking pipes above. Scavenging rats, scurry across the concrete floor.

In a far corner a single light burns, a child's Humpty Dumpty lamp, illuminating -

Denise tied to an old wooden bed. She has been stripped of her own clothes and is now wearing a little girl's dress. Her hair is tied in pigtails. She is cold and shivering.

BOOM. The basement door opens, heavy footsteps lumber down the creaking stairs. It is Tiny.

Tiny is wearing an orange T-shirt that reads " Cheap Ass Halloween costume ". For the first time we see the skin on his arms, it is severely deformed from burn scars.

He is holding a small tray. On the tray is a box of cereal, milk, a bowl and a spoon.

Tiny goes over to Denise sets down the tray and proudly displays his T-shirt.

(CONTINUED)

S. NAISH
S. NAISH
The BLACK CAT

IN MEMORY OF
DOCTOR
SATAN

Rob

My Comrade in

Southern Comic one liners.

Thank you my friend for

an experience that will make me

laugh for many moons. I sincerely

hope that you enjoy what you've created

peace love & Happiness

Walton

Goggins

Always Remember

"you goddam Grease

Monkey..."

84 CONTINUED: 84

DENISE
(hoarse and dry)
Please... Tiny, please. Let me go... help me.

Tiny stares down at Denise like a confused dog.

DENISE (CONT'D)
(crying)
Please, God please.

Tiny begins preparing her food, carefully pouring the cereal and milk into the bowl. He stirs it with the spoon.

DENISE (cont'd)
Tiny, please let me go, please.

Tiny reaches over and unties one of Denise's wrists.

DENISE (cont'd)
Thank you, thank you.

Denise carefully slips the rope off of the bedpost, freeing her other hand. She slowly sits up and starts to untie her feet.

Tinynwatches, eating his cereal.

Denise sits up, then stands, her legs are shaking.

DENISE (cont'd)
(backing away, slowly)
I'm gonna go now, I'm gonna just go home.

Tiny waves bye.

Denise backs up to the bottom of the stairs, she turns to run and bumps directly into Otis. He grabs her by the neck.

OTIS
Where the fuck you think you're a getting to?

DENISE
No, no, no, no!

Otis rushes her forward to a darkened corner, swings open a metal cage door, throws her inside.

OTIS
That's it, Tiny, everybody stays in the cage...no more playtime.
Play time is over.
TINY SHRUGS

(CONTINUED)

Huston

84 CONTINUED: 84

SEE LIVE TIGERS

Otis pulls a string and turns on a swinging ceiling light. Denise is sitting on the floor of a huge cage. She is surrounded by piles of garbage and heaps of rags.

Suddenly, three rail-thin female bodies jump out of the trash and attack Denise. She screams. Otis turns off the overhead lights.

85 INT. POLICE CAR - LATE AFTERNOON 85

Wydell and Nash are driving towards a small town gas station.

NASH
You sure this guy's supposed to ride with us...in the car?

WYDELL
Yes.

NASH
Don't seem right to me.

WYDELL
Well, it ain't up to us, Chief said pick him up and take him with us ~~on our house to house~~. Guy's an ex-cop, thinks he can help.

NASH
I just hope the old dog don't get in my way...is all I'm saying.

WYDELL
Yeah, well when you have kids you'll understand.

NASH
I ain't planning on multiplying anytime soon, Georgie. I can't limit the old Nashmaster to one lady.

WYDELL
God Forbid.

NASH
Damn straight.

WYDELL
That must be him.

SHERIFF
COUNTY
URN THIS
URN THIS F

86 EXT. GAS STATION - LATE AFTERNOON 86

A ~~rundown gas station~~ sits off to the side of the road. A filthy mechanic works on one of the many junked cars. Two fat ~~greasy men sit in~~ the hot sun playing cards.

note: speak to Dennis that his son.

A Chevy Nova sits parked next to the station. Willis leans against the side of the car drinking coffee from a Styrofoam cup.

A police cruiser pulls up. Wydell and Nash step from the car. *

WYDELL
Mr. Willis?

MR.WILLIS
Yes, sir.

WYDELL
I'm Wydell.. this is Nash. *

Wydell extends his hand, they shake hands.

NASH
Hey. *

NASH: Get off the damn car. God damn grease monkey

MR.WILLIS
George Willis...
(to Wydell)
... any leads.

WYDELL
Well, we were on our way out to run a check on couple farmhouses out on the edge of town ... closest thing we got to a lead at this point.

MR.WILLIS
That's it.

WYDELL
Well, all we know is that the kids were headed out to a spot the locals call Deadwood to play Nancy Drew with some local legend about this character everybody calls Dr. Satan.

MR.WILLIS
Dr. Satan?

A FILM BY ROB ZOMBIE
HOUSE OF 1000 CORPSES

86 CONTINUED: 86

NASH *
Yeah it's horseshit, just some boogieman
crap that the kids like scare each other
with at Halloween. *

WYDELL
Anyway, there not much else out that
way... so, I figure maybe there's a
chance the kids brokedown and found their
way over to one of the farms.

MR.WILLIS
What about the body you found?

WYDELL
(slightly surprise)
Oh, yeah, you know about that? Hmmm,
that's a strange one.

NASH *
Local girl, Karen Murphy been missing for
couple months, figured for a runaway.

MR.WILLIS
Fit the profile

NASH *
No, not really. Good kid, never been in
any trouble.

WYDELL
Her part in this I can't figure... but I
will.

MR.WILLIS
(wipes his brow)
Christ, you know it's crazy...
(gets choked up)
I lived through so many others people's
nightmares, you know. Always cool and
calm, but... but I never thought I'd be
the one needing help, ya know?

NASH *
Don't worry we'll find her. *

Willis dumps out the remaining coffee, tosses the cup into
trash and opens the back door of the Police car. He gets
inside. Wydell and Nash climb in. The car drives off. *

87 OMIT 87

88 INT. FARMHOUSE - OTIS'S ROOM - LATE AFTERNOON 88

THUMP!

CLOSE UP on a bloody bandaged face. THUMP!

As we pull back we see Jerry, completely bandaged like a mummy, strapped to a wall. His arms and legs are spread. THUMP! Knifes stick into the wall next to the body.

GRAMPA
(off screen)
God damn bitch, what the fuck are you waiting for... Charles Nelson Riley don't know shit...

We pull back further to see Otis pacing wildly back and forth in front of his TV watching MATCH GAME. Grampa sits eating a TV dinner.

OTIS
(gesturing at the TV with a knife)
Watch that bitch, she's thinking about that Klugman bangin' Brett Sommers, pick motherfucking Richard Dawson.

Otis throws the large hunting knife at the wall next to Jerry.

OTIS (CONT'D)
He's the fucking slick jack Match Game man, mamma.

GRAMPA
Where do they find these people?

A88 INT. POLICE CRUISER - LATE AFTERNOON A88

MR.WILLIS
Christ, four kids couldn't just disappear.

NASH
No they couldn't, somebody had to see something. *

MR.WILLIS
My Denise is a smart girl, she wouldn't do anything stupid and her boyfriend he always seemed like a good kid.

(CONTINUED)

THERE'S NO TURNING BACK.
HOUSE OF 1000 CORPSES
WRITTEN AND DIRECTED BY ROB ZOMBIE
DATE: 8.18.00
COMP: 4

A88 CONTINUED: A88

WYDELL
I'm sure there a logical explanation.

MR.WILLIS
I pray to God there is.

NASH
Hey boss, turn up this road. * *

MR.WILLIS
Where we headed?

WYDELL
I seem to remember another farm set way back off the road where the car was found. I'm not sure if anyone lives there anymore, but its worth a look.

89 EXT. FARMHOUSE - LATE AFTERNOON 89

Wydell's cruiser turns up the road to the Firefly farmhouse. It moves past the scarecrow and comes to a halt. The doors swing open and Wydell, Nash and Willis get out. *

Dog w Driveway

WYDELL
I'm gonna see if anybody's home. You and Mr. Willis take a look around the grounds for any sign of anything.

NASH *
Right...
(to Willis)
... come on.

Nash and Willis head off around the back of the house. *

90 INT. FARMHOUSE - KITCHEN - LATE AFTERNOON 90

Dirty dishes overflow from the rusty metal sink onto the surrounding counters. A large cat walks across piles of food left to rot on a table. Boxes of trash and old newspapers are stacked to the ceiling.

Music from a crackling radio is heard.

Mother stands stirring a large pot on the stove. A LOUD knocking interrupts her cooking. She sets down her spoon and walks to the front door.

insert [illegible] in window

Before opening the door she peeks through the curtains of a small side window. She sees Wydell and runs from the kitchen.

TREES
GARDEN
AND ALL
BIRDS
200-6 KODAK
GOLD 200-6
200-6 KODAK

A90 EXT. FARMHOUSE - LATE AFTERNOON A90

Wydell walks up the front steps.

B90 INT. FARMHOUSE - HALLWAY - LATE AFTERNOON B90

Mother runs towards a door at the end the hall. She swings open the door.

91 INT. FARMHOUSE - OTIS'S ROOM - LATE AFTERNOON 91

Mother bursts into the room.

MOTHER
Otis! Otis! Come quick, there's cops outside.

OTIS
What! God damn, how many?

GRAMPA
(watching TV)
What? How many?

OTIS
Don't worry about it.

Hugo
I Hate fucked family.
Otis
he's just a dip

Otis jumps up and goes over to an old dresser and opens a drawer and pulls out a automatic revolver.

MOTHER
I don't know. I only saw one.

flicks food at TV.

OTIS
I sure there's more than that... fucking pigs always travel in packs...
(handing the gun to Mother)
... here take this.

MOTHER
(takes the gun)
What should I do.

OTIS
Go down stairs and play nice... I'm a gonna go 'round back and handle things like I always fucking do.

Hugo throws Otis the BIRD

92 EXT. FARMHOUSE - SAME 92

Nash and Willis move through the cluttered porch of a smaller house, several doors connect to the porch.. *

92 CONTINUED: 92

NASH
(opening the door)
God damn, don't these packrats throw anything away?

Mr. Willis opens another door, nothing.

Nash moves up closer to the next door.

NASH (cont'd)
(whispering)
Hold on...someone is in here.

Nash kicks in the door. Woof! Woof! Woof! A huge dog lunges at Nash. Nash jumps back relieved to see that the dog is chained.

NASH (cont'd)
Holy shit.

MR.WILLIS
Shhhh... you hear that?

The soft sound of moaning can be heard.

NASH
Yeah, I hear it... where's it coming from.

MR.WILLIS
Over here, round back.

They move around to the back of the house to discover a tin smokehouse.

NASH
(knocking on the door)
Hey Police, anybody in there?

The moaning gets louder.

MR.WILLIS
We gotta break it open.

NASH
Now I know I ain't got a warrant to be busting open these folks' shit.

Willis picks up a broken axe handle and begins prying open the door.

MR.WILLIS
Tell it to my daughter.

(CONTINUED)

92 CONTINUED:

NASH
(grabbing hold to help)
Aw, hell.

Together they struggle to open the door.

3 INT. FARMHOUSE - SAME

Mother slowly opens the front door.

MOTHER
(trying to be sexy)
Well hello, officer.

WYDELL
(holding up a badge)
Excuse me, my name is Lt. Wydell, I like to ask you a few questions.

MOTHER
Questions? Well, heck I'll tell you anything you want to know.

WYDELL
I appreciate you cooperation. I'm looking for a missing girl...
(holds up picture)
...this girl here, Denise Willis... have you seen her.

MOTHER
Well I... mmmmm...no I ain't seen her, sorry.

She begins to close the door. Wydell stops her.

WYDELL
Please, could I please come in a talk to you for a minute. Maybe you could take a better look at the picture... might stir up something.

MOTHER
I um...no, I don't think so...

WYDELL
Please, just a minute.

MOTHER
Oh, alright... I guess I can trust you... being a man of the law and all.

She opens the door.

(CONTINUED)

HOUSE
of 1000
CORPSES

93 CONTINUED: 93

WYDELL
Thank you.

MOTHER
Oh, you are very welcome... Lord knows
how I love a man in a uniform.

She closes the door.

94 EXT. FARMHOUSE - SAME 94

Nash and Willis bust open the door to the smokehouse. Hanging *
inside is Mary. She hangs from ropes strapped to the ceiling. *
Large hunks of meat hang around her in the cramped room.

NASH *
Jesus Christ.

MR.WILLIS
Call Wydell.

95 INT. FARMHOUSE - SAME 95

Wydell and Mother sit opposite each other at the dining room. *
Pictures of the Denise and her companions are spread on the
table. Wydell takes notes as Mother talks.

WYDELL
Think... do any of these kids look
familiar in anyway?

MOTHER
No, I can't really say that I ever
seen'em before...
(points to the photo of Bill)
... he looks familiar, is he on the TV.

Suddenly, Nash's voice comes over Wydell's walkie-talkie.

NASH
Wydell.

WYDELL
Excuse me a second.

Pulls walkie-talkie from his belt to respond.

WYDELL (CONT'D)
Over.

NASH
We found one.

95 CONTINUED: 95

Click. Mother points the gun at Wydell's head and fires. He falls dead to the floor.

96 EXT. FARMHOUSE - SAME 96

Nash hears the commotion over his walkie-talkie. *

NASH *
(into walkie-talkie)
Wydell! Over! Wydell! Over!

No response.

NASH (CONT'D) *
Fuck, go to the car... call for backup.
Tell'em officer down.

MR.WILLIS
Right.

Willis runs to the car, he gets about half way there before he is hit in the back by a bullet. He stumbles and falls to his knees.

He knees silent, stunned. We hold on his face and watch as his life passes before him.

A96 In a quick MONTAGE, we see the following images flash by: A96

a. A father and daughter together in happier times.
b. A child's birthday party.
c. A baby crying.
d. Willis and his deceased wife.

Christmas morning with wife + dog

B96 Otis fires another shot. B96

Willis falls forward into the mud, dead.

Nash sees Willis fall. Before he can react a voice calls out from behind him. *

OTIS
Hands up, bitch!

Nash raises his hands. *

OTIS (CONT'D)
Turn around, real slow... piggy-pie.

Nash turns around. *

(CONTINUED)

Turning Point — For All involved
no Hope — No Rescue is Coming
time shot
time move or crane
frame rate
120 frames
Bill
super slow motion
walton

96 CONTINUED: 96

OTIS (CONT'D)
Interlock your fingers behind your head...
(Nash hesitates)
...do it!

Nash obeys.

OTIS (CONT'D)
Kneel.

Nash kneels down.

From a distance we see Otis standing over Nash, execution style. A white puff of smoke comes from Otis's gun and a distance popping sound is heard. Nash falls over on his side.

The scene fades to blood red.

C96 EXT RED HOT PUSSY LIQUORS - MIDDAY C96

A small, crummy liquor store stands next to a sleazy motel. Two homeless bums stand screaming obscenities in the parking lot.

Parked in front is Rufus's truck. Baby steps from the truck and walks toward the store, Rufus follows.

D96 INT. RED HOT PUSSY LIQUORS - MIDDAY D96

The store is decorated for Halloween.

Off to one side is a curtained room. A sign reads XXX 8mm loops, sex noises can be heard inside.

Baby and Rufus stand at the counter waiting for the CASHIER, a skinny geek with glasses, to total up their purchases. The counter is loaded with bottles.

The cashier is packing the bottles into cardboard boxes.

GOOBER
You all having a Halloween party tonight?

BABY
Now, what makes you think that, big boy?

GOOBER
You all sure are buying a whole mess of holy water for two people.

(CONTINUED)

X RATED
ACTION
BE PREPARED
TO SHOW I.D.

X RATED
ACTION
OPEN

MISSING!
Karen Murphy
CALL THE SHERIFF DEPARTMENT AT:
HI, MY NAME IS
GOOBER

D96 CONTINUED: D96

BABY
Yeah, well we like to get fucked up and do fucked up shit, you know what I mean?

GOOBER
Yeah, yeah...
(giggling)
...I liked to fuck shit up. and do some fucked up shit.

BABY
I'll bet you do... how much we owe ya...
(looks at his name tag)
...Goober?

GOOBER
(looking down at his tag)
Actually its G. Ober... Gerry Ober, but the guys drew in the other O, fucking assholes.

Find Goober

BABY
(uninterested)
Great story Goober, how much?

well the damage is quite severe

GOOBER
Ummmm... ~~two~~ one hundred and eighty-five dollars.

Baby throws down three hundred dollars.

Ain't gonna break my bank honey,

BABY
Keep the change and get yourself a new name.

my name is G.OOBER

GOOBER
Holy crap, thanks!

Rufus picks up the boxes from the counter. He and Baby start to walk away.

BABY
Come on, bro. Let's go.

Goober Thanks for curing my head cold pussy lingam

~~GOOBER~~
~~(holding out a flyer)~~
~~Hey, wait take this.~~

~~Baby stops and grabs the flyer.~~

~~BABY~~
~~What's this?~~

KODAK 400NC
5546 K150
5-11-00

D96 CONTINUED: D96

GOOBER
A missing girl. I use'ta go to school with her, she just up and disappeared one day... real weird. *

The flyer reads MISSING, KAREN MURPHY, 18. The picture on the flyer shows the smiling chubby face of a young girl.

BABY
Now isn't she a happy little cherub... o'well, I'm sure she'll turn up real soon. * * * *
(stuffs it in her pocket)
... nobody just up and disappears.

insert new clips otis playing with skin pieces

RUFUS JR.
(mutters)
Aliens.

BABY
Yeah, maybe it was fucking aliens.

E96 EXT. RED HOT PUSSY LIQUORS E96 *

Baby and Rufus exit. Rufus loads the boxes into the back of his truck. Baby stands looking off into the night and lights a cigarette. * * *

DR. WOLFENSTEIN
(V.O)
It is midnight my little boils and ghouls, the witching hour. Time for all monsters, murderers, maniacs and madmen to go to work... * * * * * * *

Along wolfenstein location

97 OMIT 97 *

98 INT. FARMHOUSE - NIGHT 98

CLOSE-UP TV

Dr. Wolfenstein is on screen smashing pumpkins with a giant hammer.

DR. WOLFENSTEIN
It is midnight my little boils and ghouls, the witching hour. Time for all monster, murderers, maniacs and madmen to go to work... so lock your doors and bolt your windows, sit back and prepare for a fright night classic...
(lightning crashes)
...The House of Frankenstein.

Wilshire Blvd
DAY: 2
DAYS: 23
HOTEL LV :
CREW CALL: 3P
SHOOTING CALL : 4P
SUNRISE: 610A
SUNSET: 736P
VEATHER: High mid 90's / 50's (varable wind)
REW REPORT TO PARKING SEE MAP
akfast @115P
TRAVEL TIME FROM HOTE
OVAL OF FIRST ASSISTANT DIRECTOR 20 Minutes
H DAY ON SET @ CALL
AGES
LOCATION
7/8
East 145th Street & Ave Q
Palmdale ,Calif
Sheri Moon fitting — RHP Pants
REMARKS
Pick Up @ Hotel
Rehearsal @ 315
ick Up @ Hotel
ck Up @ Hotel/
Rehearsal @ 8P
k Up @ Home
10P
Report to Location /
Rehearsal @ 8P
SWF
W/N
aulding's
ature watches
aulding's
ky shot
,18,50
N1

98 CONTINUED: 98

The movie begins and we move off the TV to see:

Hundreds of CANDLES are lit, illuminating everything with a flickering light. Music blares from a cheap stereo. BLACK and ORANGE PAPER STREAMERS are draped from ceiling to floor.

Dead center is a LARGE OBJECT standing seven feet tall, it is completely covered in paper Halloween decorations. A long chain connects the object up into the rafters.

This is the Halloween party from Hell.

An intoxicated Grampa, dressed as FLASH GORDON, sits in his wheelchair watching the TV, drinking MOONSHINE from an unmarked bottle.

GRAMPA
(slurred drunken yelling at the screen)
Get those motherfucker...those high water bitches and rocketship daisies... kill'em, kill'em.

CRASH! CRASH! CRASH! Tiny stands in a corner tunelessly banging on a large oil drum. He is dressed like a low-budget BATMAN, in grey long johns and a black bat mask and cape.

A drunk Rufus, wearing a bloody police uniform, stands on a table SHOUTING along to the music through a POLICE MEGAPHONE.

Mother and Baby, both dressed as SUPERHEROES, dance around the covered object. Both are swigging moonshine from jugs.

RUFUS JR.
(shouting through ~~megaphone~~) cut megaphone
Show me, show me, show me, show me!

Mother and Baby start TEARING AWAY the paper covering from the object in the middle of the room. They RIP at the paper, spinning and dancing around in a wild pagan ritual.

As the shreds of colored paper falls to the floor we see: Denise, Jerry and Mary tied back to back hanging from a chain, each are dressed in a different animal costume. Denise is a pig, Jerry is a donkey and Mary is a rabbit. They are gagged.

Mother and Baby laugh at their helpless victims, splashing moonshine in their faces.

harness
suspend from ceiling
find rigging points

BABY
Drink up, it's party time.

(CONTINUED)

MOTHER
Enjoy your last night...
(looking around)
... where's Otis?

BABY
Oh, he's coming he got something real special this year.

Rufus jumps down begins to spin the bound captives around and around.

RUFUS JR.
Otis, Otis, Otis, Otis!

MOTHER
Quiet, quiet you know he won't come down with all this hoop-dee-doo bouncing off the walls. Now, calm down.

GRAMPA
I shot an elephant in my pajamas this morning... how he got in my pajamas I'll never know.

BABY
Grampa, shhhhhhhhh.

GRAMPA
Then we tried to remove the tusks, but they were embedded in so firmly that we couldn't budge'em.

MOTHER
(gesturing at Grampa)
Let him finish.

GRAMPA
Of course, in Alabama the Tuscaloosa, but that's entirely irrelephant.

The room goes silent. All eyes are focused on the stairs.

A robed figure, Otis, appears at the top of the stairs, he begins to descend.

Rufus waits at the bottom of the stairs. As Otis reaches the last step Rufus hands him the megaphone.

Denise, Mary and Jerry struggle to watch as they in turn rotate pass the scene unfolding.

(CONTINUED)

YOU KEEP ME
IN STITCHES

98 CONTINUED: 98

OTIS
(through the megaphone)
I'm the one who brings the Christmas candy...now tell me
(pauses and raises his arms)
... Who's your Daddy?

Otis walks closer to the rotating captives.

OTIS (CONT'D)
I'm the one who brings the devil's brandy...
(waits)

MOTHER
Who's your Daddy!

OTIS
Yes! I'm the one who beats you when your bad...

BABY
Who's your Daddy!

MOTHER
Who's your Daddy!

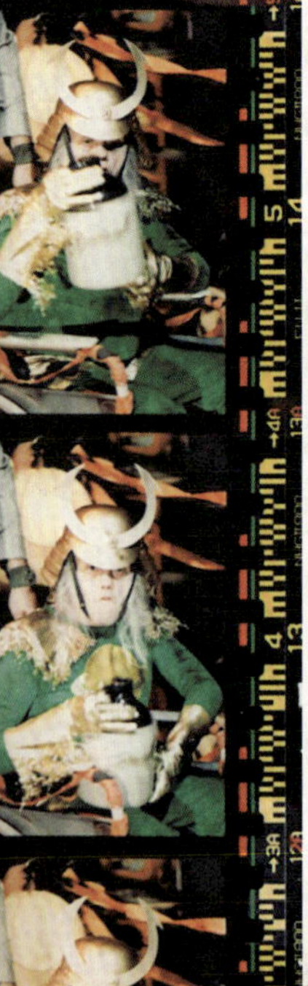

Otis stop the spinning of his prisoners and stands directly before Denise.

He drops his robe, underneath he is wearing a SUIT OF SKIN sewn together from pieces of Denise's father.

Denise stares in horror, tears stream down her cheeks, barely able to comprehend the madness around her.

Otis moves in close and licks her across the face.

OTIS
~~I'm the one who loves you when your fucking dead!~~
come sweety give the old man some sugar

Everyone chants "Who's your Daddy"?

OTIS (CONT'D)
(imitating Willis)
Now, I say my little darlings...
(rotates the chain to Mary)
maybe prancing around where you don't belong ain't such a winner of an idea... is it?
(slaps Mary across the face)

(CONTINUED)

5546 THE HOUSE OF 1000 CORPSES

98 CONTINUED: 98

Slowly turns the chain to face Jerry.

OTIS (CONT'D)
And you the great rusher of fools, what were you after...
(slaps Jerry)
Huh, speak to me...
(slaps him again)
Oh, that's right Dr.Satan... everybody got to know about Dr. Satan, Jesus Christ let the old dog rest for fuck sake, he's already got one foot in the grave and the other's tap dancing around the edge...
(gets nose to nose with Jerry)
...well, I can see the disappointment, on your sad little puppy face...so I'm gonna do you a favor, a big, big favor. You owe me, boy. I'm gonna let you meet the old bastard.

GRAMPA
That's a horses's ass alright, I told you.

Jerry eyes widen in fear.

OTIS
Baby, roll that old love machine over here, so this boy can meet his hero.

Baby rolls Grampa over to Jerry.

OTIS (CONT'D)
(lifts his skin mask)
You see it's all true, the boogie man is real and you found him...
(Jerry stares in shock)
... why so sad? Isn't this what you begged for? There he is the living legend himself, ta da Dr.Satan. Now, don't get shy on me... ask your hero some questions, don't blow this last in a lifetime opportunity.

GRAMPA
Zarkoff, I will conquer the sea, the air, the earth... the universe.

Mother moves in close to Jerry.

MOTHER
Look at the way he lights up... Grampa just loves meeting his fans.

(CONTINUED)

OTIS. lifts mask: It's all True the Boogeyman real and you found him

Hugo Not Dr. Satan

98 CONTINUED: 98

Otis grabs Jerry's cheeks and make his face move like a ventriloquist dummy, provides Jerry's voice.

OTIS
Aw gee whiz, I'm so excited... I really think your the coolest... your tops on the playground cooler than the Fonzie.

Baby grabs Mary and does the same ventriloquist routine.

BABY
Oh, oh pick me, pick me... I have a question.

Baby rotates Mary around to where Grampa is seated.

BABY (CONT'D)
(squeezing Mary's face, hard)
I was wondering Mr.Satan sir, do you like to kiss on the first date or is that considered slutty?

GRAMPA
What the fuck are you saying? Who the hell is talking to me?

Tiny, growing restless, he begins banging on his metal drum. KLANG - KLANG - KLANG. Rufus joins in clamping his hands.

MOTHER
Come on, my babies are getting restless.

RUFUS JR.
Dump in the pit, dump in the pit, dump the pit.

Mother, Baby, Grampa join in chanting with Rufus.

OTIS
Alright, alright. Cut'em down, it's time they get what they came here for.

99 EXT. FIELD - NIGHT 99

A heavy fog hovers over the dense growth of the field. In the distance silhouetted by moonlight a gruesome caravan slowly moves through the night. *

Otis, lantern in hand, leads the way. Followed by Baby and Mother. Next Rufus holds the leash connected to Jerry, Denise and Mary. *

99 CONTINUED: 99

Bringing up the rear, Tiny, Shotgun focused on the prisoners, and Grampa. He waves a flashlight back and forth like a search beam. *

The group comes to a halt at a huge wooden structure.

OTIS
(handing Baby the lantern)
Hold this.

Tiny already at structure

OTIS (CONT'D)
Point it over here.

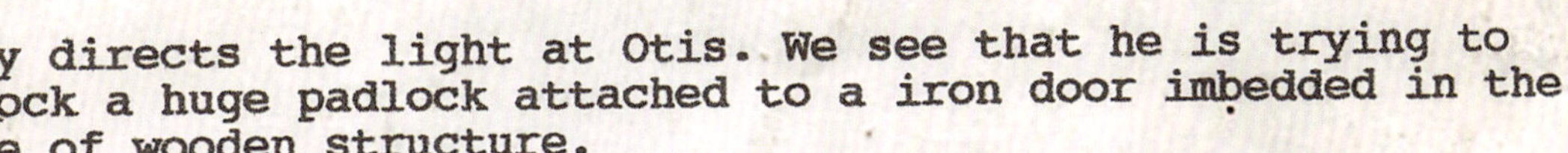

Baby directs the light at Otis. We see that he is trying to unlock a huge padlock attached to a iron door imbedded in the base of wooden structure.

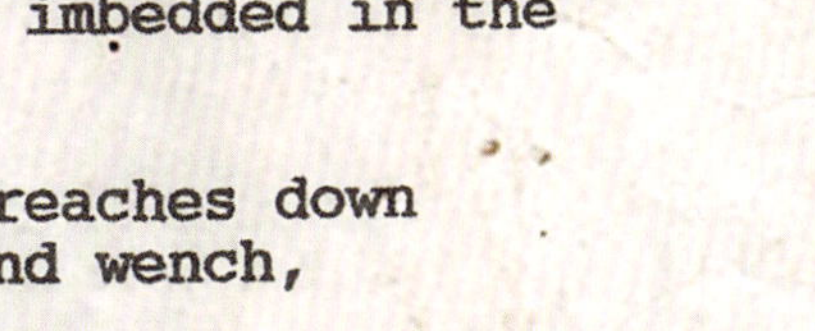

Otis unlocks the door and swings it open. He reaches down into the blackness and pulls up a iron hook and wench, attached to the hook is chain.

Otis parts a section of the overgrown grass next to the pit to reveal a rusty metal crank. He begins to turn the crank. Slowly, from out of the pit, rises a coffin hanging from the end of the chain.

Otis pulls the coffin over and lays it flat on the ground. He flips open the lid.

OTIS (CONT'D)
Hey happy-boy, step your ass up here.

Rufus cuts loose Jerry, but holds him steady by the neck.

BABY
Take his gag out, it's more fun with the screaming.

MOTHER
Yeah, I like the screaming too...it's so much more exciting.

Rufus cut loose the gag.

JERRY
Please don't kill us, please don't kill us.

BABY
(imitating Jerry)
Please don't kill us, please don't kill us.

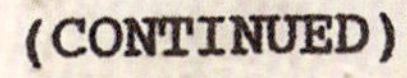

(CONTINUED)

99 CONTINUED: 99

OTIS
Bitch, shut you mouth and get your shit
in the box.

JERRY
Let us go, please... let the girls go.

BABY
(imitating Jerry)
Let us go, please... let the girls go.

Otis pulls out a gun and points it at Jerry.

OTIS
Get in... now!

MOTHER
Wait, I want to say good-bye.

Mother grabs Jerry by the collar and gives him a big kiss.

MOTHER (CONT'D)
(to Jerry)
Bye sweety , we could of been great
together.

JERRY
Please, let us go, we won't tell anybody.

MOTHER
Aw, honey you know I can't do that. mamma drops Jerry/

BABY
We won't tell anybody.

Otis cocks the pistol. Jerry starts to slowly move towards the coffin.

OTIS
Christ, ain't this fucking a hoot...
alright mamma, I ain't got all fucking
night.

JERRY
Please, please this is insane. You can't
do this.

Rufus pushes Jerry into the coffin.

OTIS
It is and I can... next.

EXEC. PRODUCER: Andy Gives
Courtesy Breakfast Shuttle From Hotel 410F
ves @ 440P
SHOOTING CALL : 545P
SUNRISE: 610A
SUNSET: 736P
WEATHER: High mid 90's / 50's (varable wind)
CREW REPORT TO PARKING SEE MAP
Breakfast
TRAVEL TIME FROM HOTEL 20 Minutes
NO VISTORS WITHOUT APPROVAL OF FIRST ASSISTANT DIRECTOR
NG FOR ALL CREW EACH DAY ON SET @ CALL
D/N
PAGES
LOCATION
D2
3/8
East 145th Street & Ave Q
Palmdale ,Calif
N1
5/8
N1
3/8
ZOMBIE
Ext-Spaulding's Phone Booth
22,24,A25,C25
4
Ext-Spaulding's Phone Booth
27
1,2,3,4
28
2,11
29
1,2,3,4,11
Fri May 12
ZOMBIE

99 CONTINUED: 99

Denise starts kicking and fighting with Rufus. Rufus tries to hold her steady, when suddenly Mary breaks free and starts to run.

Insert Otis Super 8

Hunting humans ain't nothing but nothing. They all run like scared little rabbits. Run, rabbit run

OTIS (CONT'D)
(laughs and raises his pistol)
Where's she think she's a gonna get to... *
(laughing) *
She's gonna run all the way home.

BABY
No! Let me get her...
(turns to mother)
... Ma, Otis is having all the fun... can I get her.

MOTHER
That's true, Otis... not that we're having a bad time, but...

OTIS
(rolls his eyes)
Well, go get her.

Baby jumps with excitement and runs off across the field after Mary.

Mary trips and falls over a small gravestone into thick mud. She gets up and stumbles back into a wooden cross. She tears the gag from her mouth and gasps for air. *

BABY
(off screen)
There once was a woman who lived with her daughter in a cabbage garden.

Mary turns towards the voice but sees nothing but wooden crosses. She is in a homemade cemetery.

BABY (CONT'D)
... along came a rabbit and ate up all the cabbages, the woman said...

Mary turns 360 degrees, but finds nothing.

BABY (CONT'D)
... "Go into the garden and drive out the rabbit...

THUD! Mary is hit from behind, she falls forward. Baby JUMPS on top of her and sits on her back. Baby is holding a large hunting knife.

99 CONTINUED: 99

BABY (CONT'D)
"Shoo! Shoo!" said the maiden...

Mary screams in pain, as Baby PLUNGES the knife into her. Baby STABS Mary again and again and again. Mary lets out on long gurgling scream, then goes silent.

BABY (CONT'D)
... "Come maiden," said the rabbit...
(leans down)
... sit on my tail and go with me to my rabbit hutch.

Baby, covered in blood, licks the knife clean.

100 EXT. PIT - NIGHT

~~Otis~~ Rufus shoves Denise into the coffin with Jerry and locks the lid shut. Through a CROSS-SHAPED OPENING in the coffin we see them crushed together.

Rufus LOWERS the coffin into the pit. Once the coffin is inside Otis slams the door shut.

Otis opens a small window in the door and lowers in a lantern and a small tape recorder playing music.

101 INT. PIT - NIGHT

Enter Hell. The dim light of the lantern shines off the slimy wet filth of the rotted wood walls. The stench of death and decay hangs heavy in the thin air.

Denise and Jerry, cold and shivering, hang half submerged in thick maggot infested sludge. Bits of animal and human skeletons float in the muck, broken bones lay in piles along the walls.

102 INT. COFFIN - NIGHT

Through the dim light, we see the tightly packed forms of Jerry and Denise.

DENISE
(hysterical)
We've got get out of here, we got get out of here.

JERRY
Think, think. Try to open the lid, try to kick a hole in the wood.

PANAVISION

102 CONTINUED: 102

DENISE
(crying)
I can't... I can't move my arms. I hurt so much.

JERRY
I know, but we can make it out of here. We can do it.

Boom! A LOUD THUMP is heard against the side of the coffin.

JERRY (CONT'D)
That was good Babe, just keep doing that.

BOOM, BOOM, BOOM.

DENISE
That's not me. I didn't... I'm not doing it.

Otis lowers lantern + tape recorder into pit.

JERRY
Someone is out there...
(shouting)
... help, we in here.

Bury me in the Nameless Grave

DENISE
Help, help us.

Suddenly, an arm breaks through the side of the coffin. Another smashes through the top of the lid. The coffin begins to violently shake. Denise screams.

Another reaches through grabbing her feet. SMASH ! The coffin is ripped apart and Jerry is pulled away from the destruction.

He lets out a quick scream before disappearing into the darkness.

DENISE (CONT'D)
Jerry! Jerry! Jerry!

103 INT. FARMHOUSE - LIVINGROOM - NIGHT 103

The spastic light of TV static strobes across the sleeping face of Grampa. Beside him, Mother sleeps peacefully.

104 EXT. BARN - NIGHT 104

The rain has stopped. Tiny opens the doors to the barn. He goes inside. He exits a few moments later dragging a huge wooden stake. He sets the stake down and carefully closes the barn doors. He then picks up the stake and drags it away.

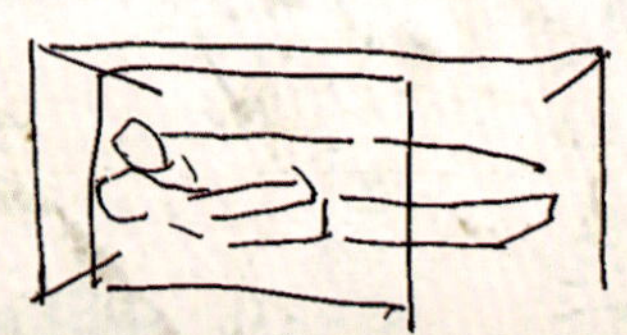

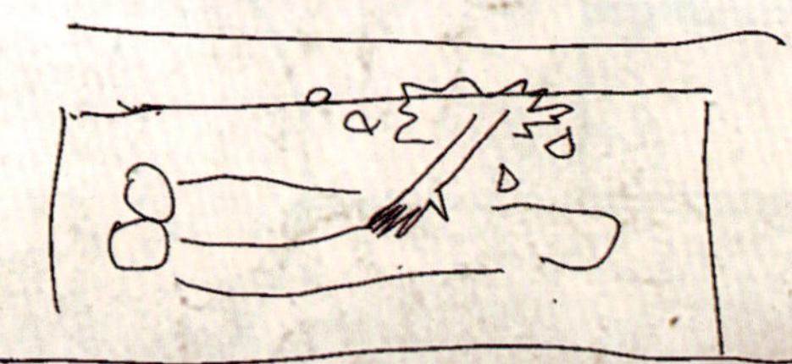

5546 K1034
5546 K1035

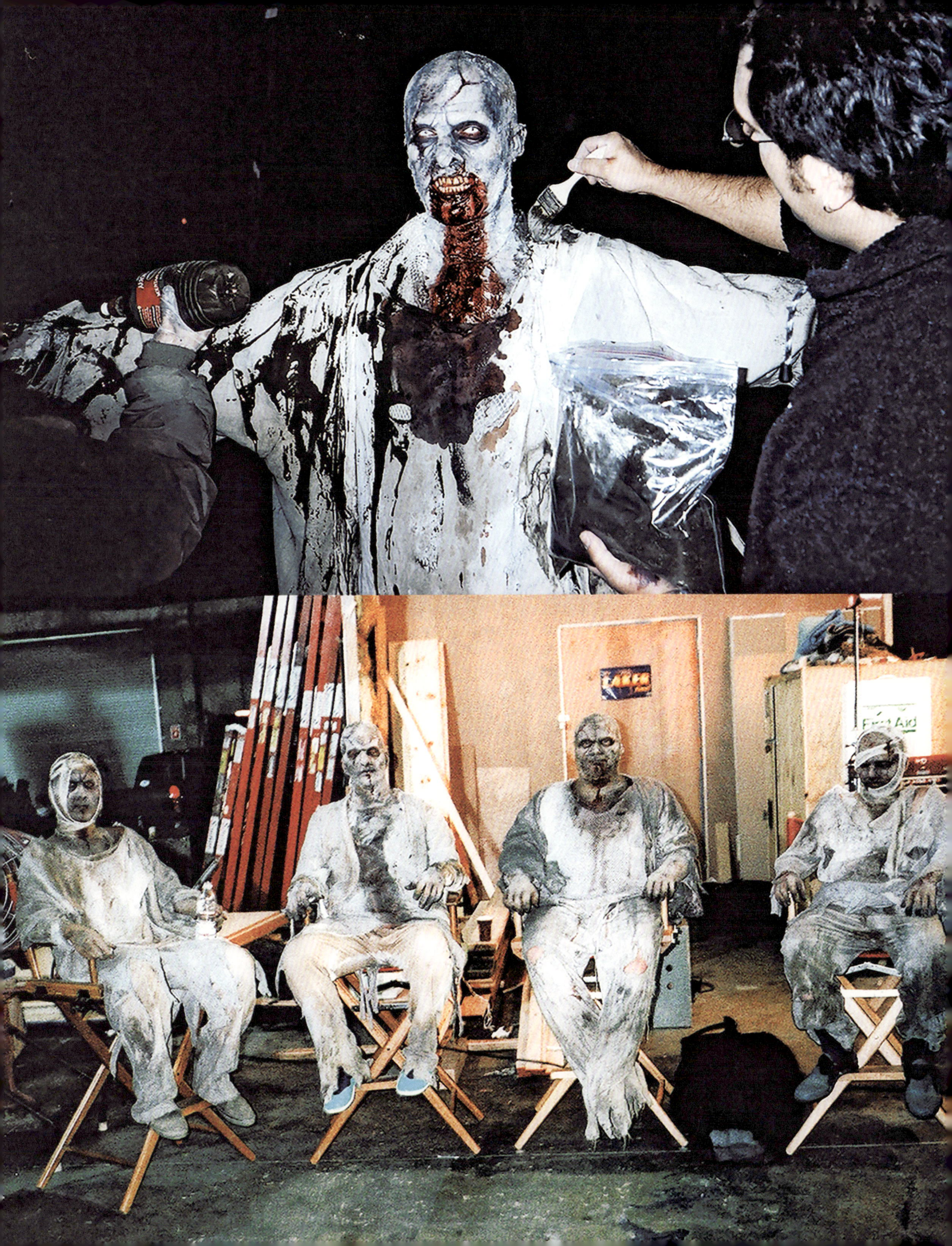
First Aid

105 EXT. BACKYARD - NIGHT

Behind the farmhouse is a camouflage jungle, an intricate system of ropes and netting is strung together to hide the many automobiles beneath.

Rufus moves through the jungle. He stops and begins to remove the netting from a car, it is Wydell's police cruiser. He climbs inside the car, puts on Wydell's policeman's hat and starts the engine. He drives off.

106 INT. POLICE CAR - NIGHT

Rufus is driving like a maniac through the open farmland. He turns on the overhead flashing lights.

107 EXT. FIELDS - NIGHT

The police cruiser twists and turns in the barren fields.

108 INT. PIT - NIGHT

Denise stands knee deep in the sludge. Broken bits of the coffins remains are scattered around her.

DENISE
Jerry please answer me.

A soft moaning sound is here coming from the other end of the pit.

DENISE (CONT'D)
Jerry...
(moving slowly forward)
... is that you?

Denise cautiously makes her way out of the sludge on to dry ground. She moves toward the bend at the end of the tunnel. As she approaches, the moaning sound gets louder. She turns the corner to see :

TWO PALE FIGURES in filthy hospital gowns hunched over a shadowy object. Denise gasps. They turn towards Denise, revealing the partially devoured dead body of Jerry.

The two bone-white ghouls are dripping with Jerry's blood, they stare at Denise, then return to their prey.

Denise screams in horror and runs, turning down another twist in the underground maze. She turns the corner and runs straight into SEVERAL SLOW MOVING GHOULS. The ghouls are of the same deathly white complexion, hairless with flaked cracking skin. Their yellow eyes shine in the darkness.

(CONTINUED)

108 CONTINUED: 108

They reach for her, but she breaks free and continues to run into the endless stretch of tunnels before her.

109 EXT. GRAVEYARD - NIGHT 109

Primitive wooden crosses form a circle around a burnt piece of land, approximately twenty feet in diameter.

Laying flat in the center is the large stake, Mary's body is draped across it. Tiny is securing her to the stake with rope, then places a pumpkin over her head. *

110 INT. POLICE CAR - NIGHT 110

Through the windshield, we see Baby jumping and dancing in the fields with several large dogs. She is firing a gun as she dances.

111 EXT. FIELD - NIGHT 111

Baby sees the car and raises her gun. She aims it at the car driver. She waits, as the car gets closer she sees the face of Rufus behind the wheel. She lowers the gun and begins to laugh.

The car stops and Baby climbs into the passenger's seat. The car drives off.

112 EXT. GRAVEYARD - NIGHT 112

Tiny lifts the stake with Mary firmly strapped in place. He implants it into the ground. Her body hangs like a doll. Tiny opens a gasoline can and begins splashing gas onto the stake.

113 EXT. FIELD - NIGHT 113

Otis, face painted like a SKULL and wearing a priest's robe, walks solemnly through the tall grass.

114 INT. PIT - NIGHT 114

Denise wanders lost through the endless tunnels of the pit. In the distance she hears high pitch animal sounds. *

A GHOUL rises up from the sludge behind Denise. It stands silent. It reaches out a BONEY HAND with long curled fingernails and grabs her hair. Denise screams and tries to pull away. The ghoul grabs her with his other hand and pulls her closer, CLAWING at her face.

Denise fights her way free, but loses her footing and falls backwards, slipping under the sludge. She quickly resurfaces and starts to run.

BLACK CAT

115 EXT. GRAVEYARD - NIGHT 115

Otis, stands in front of the bound Mary.

Tiny stands behind him holding a lit torch.

116 EXT. FIELD - NIGHT 116

The police car drives wildly through the fields.

117 INT. POLICE CAR - NIGHT 117

Baby motions to Rufus to steer the car towards the fire.

118 INT. PIT - NIGHT 118

A beaten Denise struggles down a long tunnel. She gets to the end, she crashes through the floor into deep sludge. Behind her, FIVE GHOULS move silently towards her blocking her only exit.

The ghouls move in closer. Denise frantically looks for an escape, nailed into the wall next to her are planks of wood forming a ladder.

The ghouls are only a few yards away. Denise climbs up the ladder. They move in, clawing at her legs and feet trying to pull her down. Denise digs at the wood and mud ceiling above her trying to break free.

Denise is bleeding severely from the wounds in her legs. She digs wildly at the ceiling, suddenly a board falls free and mud rains down to reveal :

STARS, the sky above shines through the hole. Denise smashes her fists at the rotted wood planks, pulling free another piece.

With all her might Denise grabs hold and pulls herself up through the opening.

119 EXT. PIT - NIGHT 119

Denise fights her way through the earth and pulls her body up into the night air. The cool air rushes to her lungs. She crawls free of the hole, gasping for air.

She is safe, suddenly... SMASH! A ghoul has broken through the surface. He grabs Denise by the leg and begins to pull her back into the hole.

Denise scream and begins kicking violently at the ghoul. She breaks and crawls from the ghoul's reach.

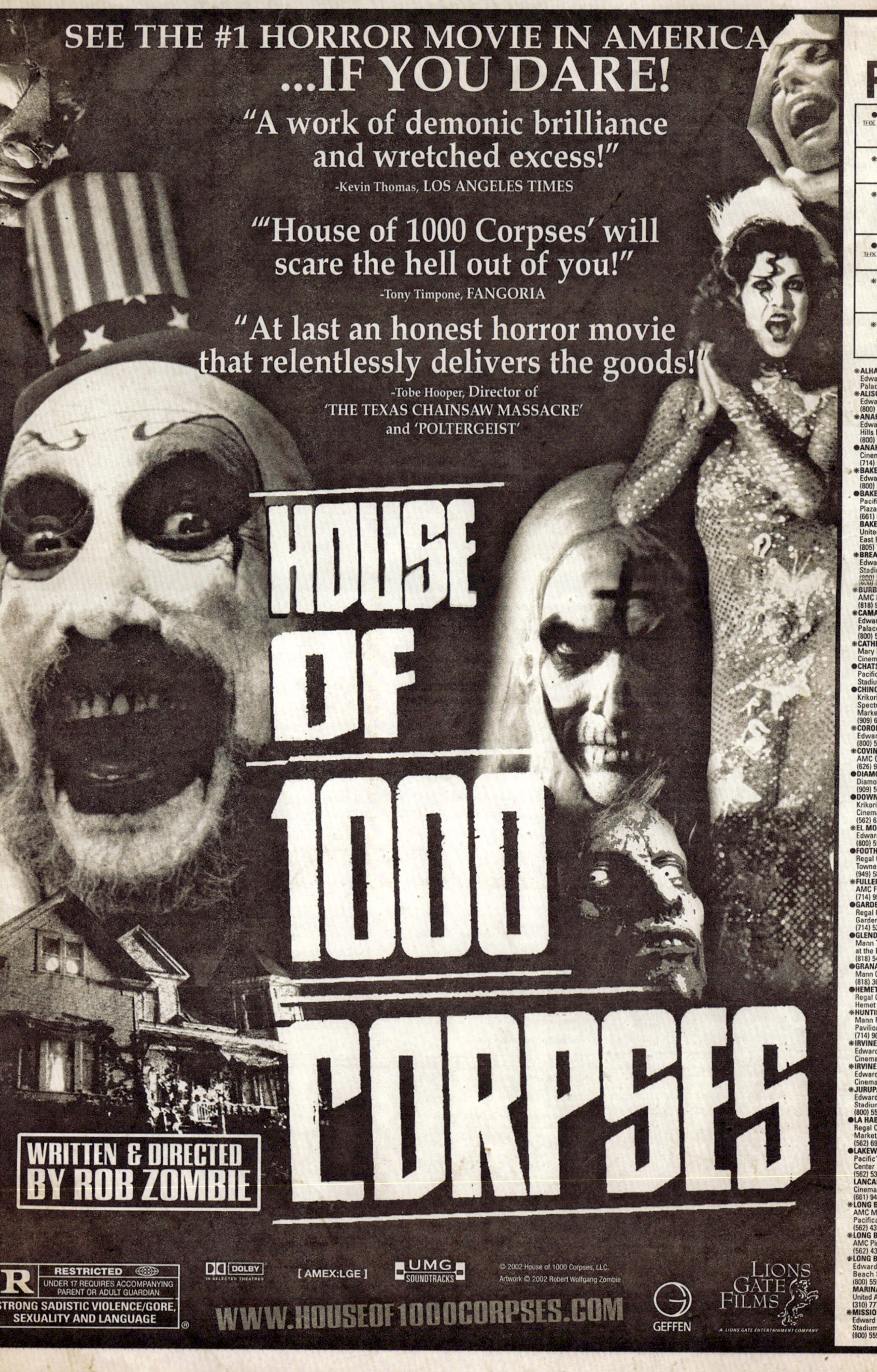

NOW PLAYING!

●**HOLLYWOOD**
THX Mann Chinese 6 (323) 777-FILM #059
Daily: 12:40 • 3:00 • 5:20 • 7:50 • 10:10
Fri. & Sat. Late Show: 12:40 am

✱**BEVERLY HILLS**
AMC Beverly Connection (310) 659-5911
Daily: 2:40 • 5:00 • 7:30 • 9:40

✱**UNIVERSAL CITY**
Loews Cineplex Universal Studios Cinema
(800) 555-TELL
Daily: 11:30 • 2:20 • 4:50 • 7:20 • 9:50
Fri. & Sat. Late Show: 12:10 am

●**SANTA MONICA**
THX Mann Criterion 6 (310) 248-MANN #019
Daily: 12:00 • 2:30 • 5:00 • 7:25 • 10:00

✱**WEST LOS ANGELES**
The Bridge Cinema De Lux (310) 568-3375
Daily: 12:45 • 3:00 • 5:15 • 7:30 • 9:45
Fri. & Sat. Late Show: 12:00 am

✱**BALDWIN HILLS**
Magic Theatres at Crenshaw Plaza
(800) 555-TELL
Daily: 11:10 • 1:50 • 4:30 • 7:10 • 9:55

✱**ALHAMBRA** Edwards Atlantic Palace 10 (800) 555-TELL
✱**ALISO VIEJO** Edwards Aliso Viejo 20 (800) 555-TELL
✱**ANAHEIM HILLS** Edwards Anaheim Hills Festival (800) 555-TELL
●**ANAHEIM HILLS** Cinema City Theatres (714) 970-6700
✱**BAKERSFIELD** Edwards Bakersfield 14 (800) 555-TELL
●**BAKERSFIELD** Pacific's Valley Plaza Stadium 16 (661) 833-2200
BAKERSFIELD United Artists East Hills Mall (805) 777-FILM #063
✱**BREA** Edwards Brea Stadium 22 (800) 555-TELL
✱**BURBANK** AMC Burbank 14 (818) 953-9800
✱**CAMARILLO** Edwards Camarillo Palace 12 Cinemas (800) 555-TELL
✱**CATHEDRAL CITY** Mary Pickford 14 Cinemas (760) 328-7100
●**CHATSWORTH** Pacific's Winnetka Stadium 21 (818) 501-5121
●**CHINO** Krikorian's Chino Spectrum Marketplace 12 (909) 628-1500
✱**CORONA** Edwards Big Corona 15 (800) 555-TELL
✱**COVINA** AMC Covina 30 (626) 974-8600
●**DIAMOND BAR** Diamond Bar 8 (909) 595-8787
●**DOWNEY** Krikorian's Downey Cinema 10 (562) 622-3999
✱**EL MONTE** Edwards El Monte 8 (800) 555-TELL
●**FOOTHILL RANCH** Regal Cinemas Foothill Towne Center 22 (949) 588-9333
✱**FULLERTON** AMC Fullerton 20 (714) 992-6000
●**GARDEN GROVE** Regal Cinemas Garden Grove 16 (714) 534-4777
●**GLENDALE** THX Mann Theatres at the Exchange (818) 549-0045
●**GRANADA HILLS** THX Mann Granada Hills 9 (818) 363-3679
●**HEMET** Regal Cinemas Hemet 12 (909) 658-3356
✱**HUNTINGTON BEACH** Mann Pierside Pavilion 6 (714) 969-3151
✱**IRVINE** Edwards 21 MegaPlex Cinemas (800) 555-TELL
✱**IRVINE** Edwards Westpark Cinema 8 (800) 555-TELL
✱**JURUPA VALLEY** Edwards Jurupa Stadium 14 (800) 555-TELL
●**LA HABRA** Regal Cinemas La Habra Marketplace 16 (562) 690-7469
●**LAKEWOOD** Pacific's Lakewood Center Stadium 16 (562) 531-9580
LANCASTER Cinemark Lancaster (661) 940-1136
✱**LONG BEACH** AMC Marina Pacifica 12 (562) 435-4AMC
✱**LONG BEACH** AMC Pine Square 16 (562) 435-4AMC
✱**LONG BEACH** Edwards Long Beach Stadium 26 (800) 555-TELL
MARINA DEL REY United Artists Cinemas (310) 777-FILM #301
✱**MISSION VIEJO** Edward Kaleidoscope Stadium 10 Cinemas (800) 555-TELL
●**MONROVIA** Krikorian's Monrovia Cinema 12 (626) 305-7469
●**MORENO VALLEY** Canyon Springs (909) 782-0800
●**MURRIETA** The Movie Experience 17 at California Oaks (909) 698-7800
●**NORTH HOLLYWOOD** Century 8 Theatres (818) 508-6004
✱**NORWALK** AMC Norwalk 20 (562) 864-5678
✱**ONTARIO** AMC Ontario Mills 30 (909) 484-3000
✱**ONTARIO** Edwards Mountain Village Stadium 14 Cinemas (800) 555-TELL
✱**ONTARIO** Edwards Ontario 22 (800) 555-TELL
●**ORANGE** Century Stadium 25 (714) 532-9533
✱**ORANGE** AMC 30 at the Block (714) 769-4AMC
PALMDALE Antelope Valley 10 (661) 267-4940
●**PARAMOUNT** Bianchi Theatres (562) 630-SHOW
✱**PASADENA** AMC Old Pasadena 8 (626) 585-8900
●**PERRIS** The Ultraplex ™ 10 at Perris Plaza (909) 943-6425
POMONA Indian Hill Cinema (909) 469-6550
✱**PUENTE HILLS** AMC Puente Hills 20 (626) 810-5566
●**REDLANDS** Krikorian's Redlands Cinema 14 (909) 793-6393
✱**REDONDO BEACH** AMC Galleria at So. Bay 16 (310) 793-7077
RIVERSIDE United Artists Park Sierra (909) 777-FILM#311
●**RIVERSIDE** CinemaStar Ultraplex ™ 18 at Mission Grove (909) 789-8483
●**SAN BERNARDINO** CinemaStar Empire 20 (909) 386-7050
✱**SAN LUIS OBISPO** Fremont (805) 541-2141
✱**SANTA CLARITA** Edwards Canyon Country Stadium 10 Cinemas (800) 555-TELL
●**SHERMAN OAKS** Pacific's Galleria Stadium 16 (818) 501-5121
✱**SIMI VALLEY** Regal Cinemas Civic Center 16 (805) 526-9800
●**SOUTH BAY** Pacific's Beach Cities Cinema 16 (310) 607-0007
✱**SOUTH GATE** Edwards South Gate Stadium 20 (800) 555-TELL
●**TEMECULA** The Movie Experience At Tower Plaza (909) 698-7800
●**THOUSAND OAKS** THX Mann Janss Marketplace 9 (805) 374-9656
✱**TORRANCE** AMC Rolling Hills 20 (310) 289-4AMC
●**VAN NUYS** Mann Plant 16 (818) 779-0323
●**VENTURA** Mann Buenaventura (805) 658-6544
VICTORVILLE Bear Valley 10 (760) 241-8400
✱**WEST COVINA** Edwards West Covina 18 at The Lakes (800) 555-TELL
●**WHITTIER** Whittier Village (562) 907-3300

✱Presented in DOLBY
●Presented in DOLBY SR

120 EXT. GRAVEYARD - NIGHT 120

Rufus and Baby have pulled the police cruiser up by the stake. They get out, Baby jumps up on the hood. *

Otis finishes his sermon, he raises his arm. Tiny raises the torch. Otis drops his arm signaling Tiny. Tiny throws the torch onto the stake. The stake ignites into a huge FIREBALL.

121 EXT. FIELD - NIGHT 121

Denise pulls herself to her feet and begins to run. The flaming object burns in the distance behind her. Denise stumbles towards the road on two badly injured legs.

122 EXT. GRAVEYARD - NIGHT 122

Rufus, Tiny and Baby jump up and down in celebration, smashing the police car. Otis stands transfixed by the flames before him.

123 EXT. ROAD - NIGHT 123

Denise makes her way out onto the road. No cars are in sight. In the distance headlights break through the darkness. Denise stands in the middle of the road.

convertible

The TRUCK comes into view, it is a small cube truck. Denise stands in the headlights, waving her arms for it to stop. The truck comes to a halt.

She runs towards the passengers side door and climbs in.

124 INT. TRUCK - NIGHT 124

Behind the wheel of the truck is Spaulding. Denise is shaking from shock. *

DENISE
Go, go! Drive... drive!

SPAULDING *
Hold on girly, what's the problem?

DENISE
(becoming hysterical)
Murdering... blood and Jerry... (starts to cry uncontrollably
...monsters... I... I... I got away...

"HOUSE OF 1000 CORPSES"

GIRLS
"BUXOM BEAUTEASE"
GIRLS
HARDCORE
SEX
ACTION
GIRLS GALORE
25¢
LAFFS AND GAGS
SEX
"Bizarre Party"
"Battling Babes"
"Lace Me Tighter"
XXX
MOVIES
8mm
loops
25¢
GIRLS
GIRLS
GIRLS
XXX
FULL OF ACTION!

HOUSE OF 1000 CORPSES

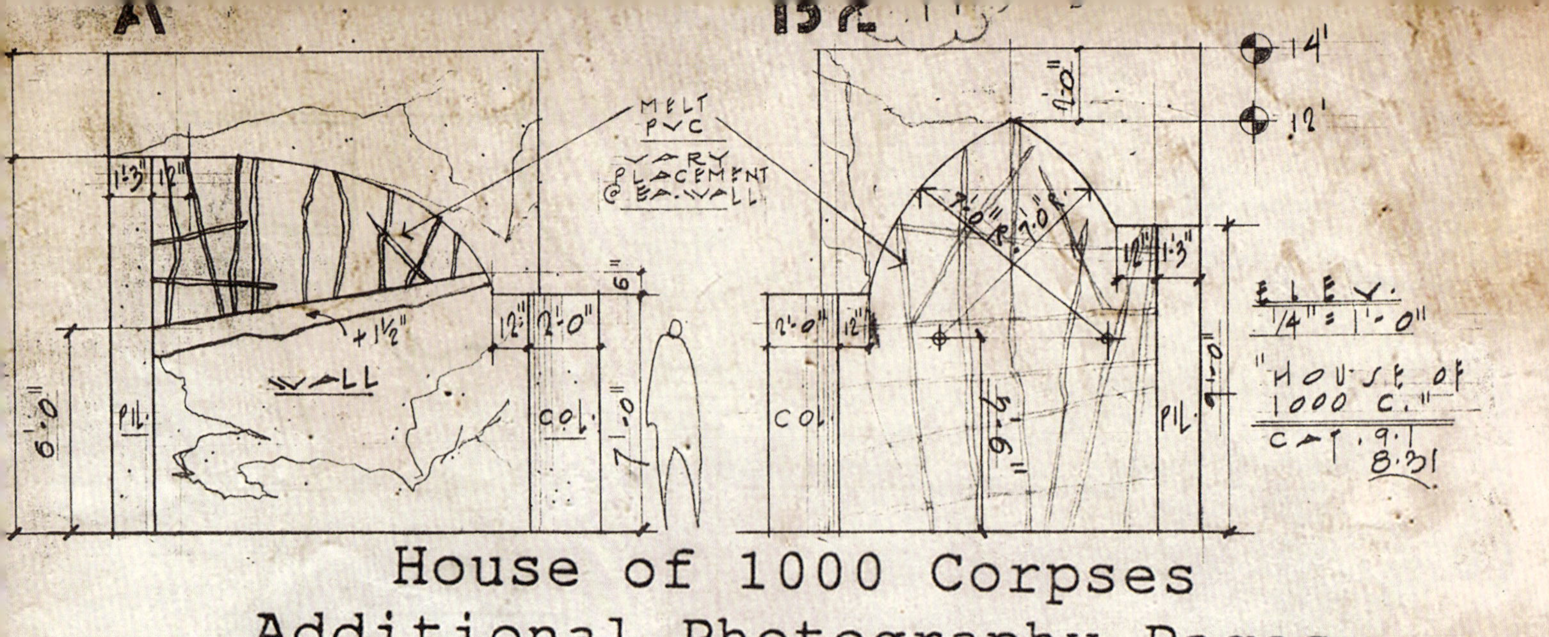

House of 1000 Corpses
Additional Photography Pages

Rev. September 14, 2000

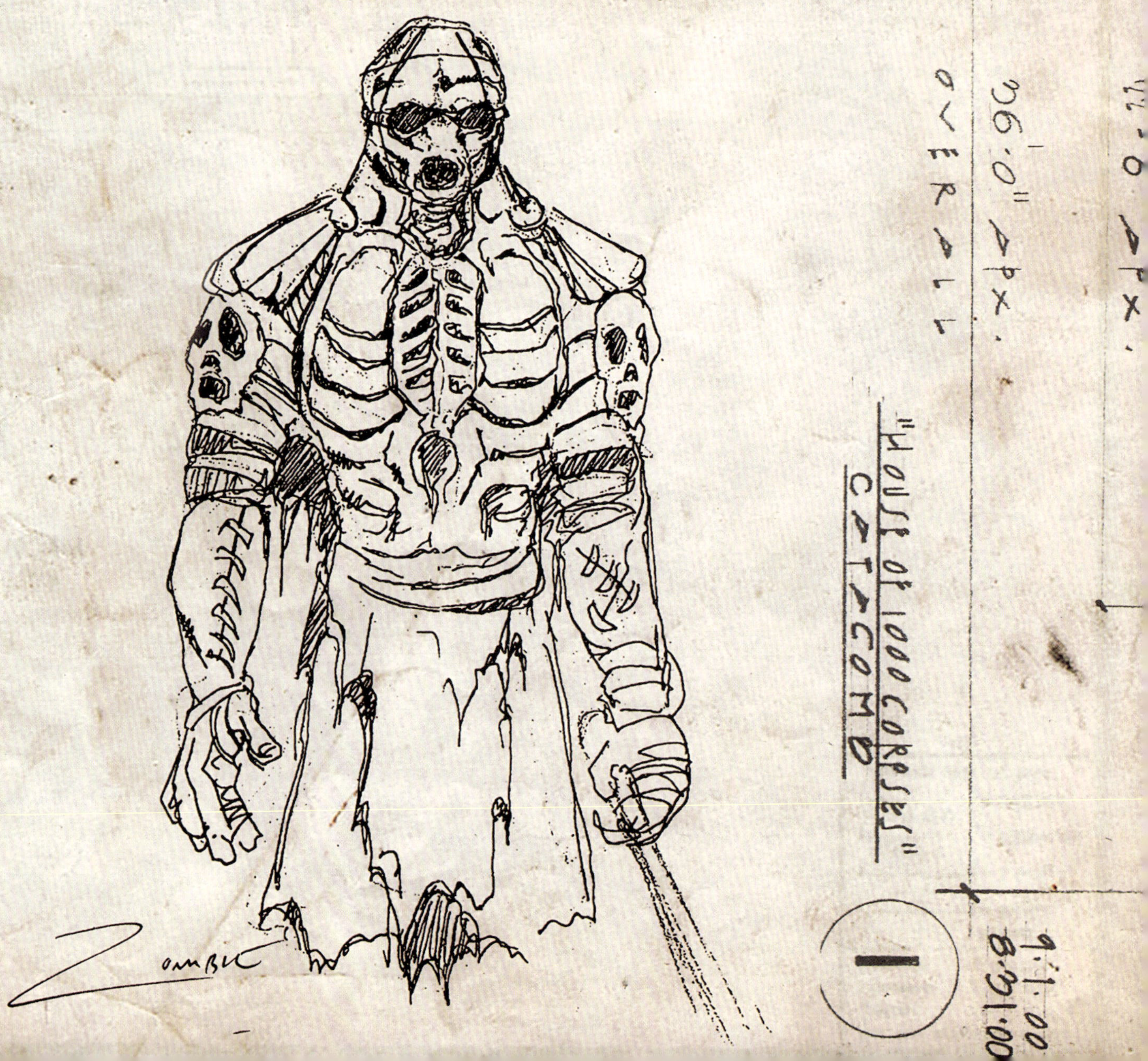

BLACK CAT

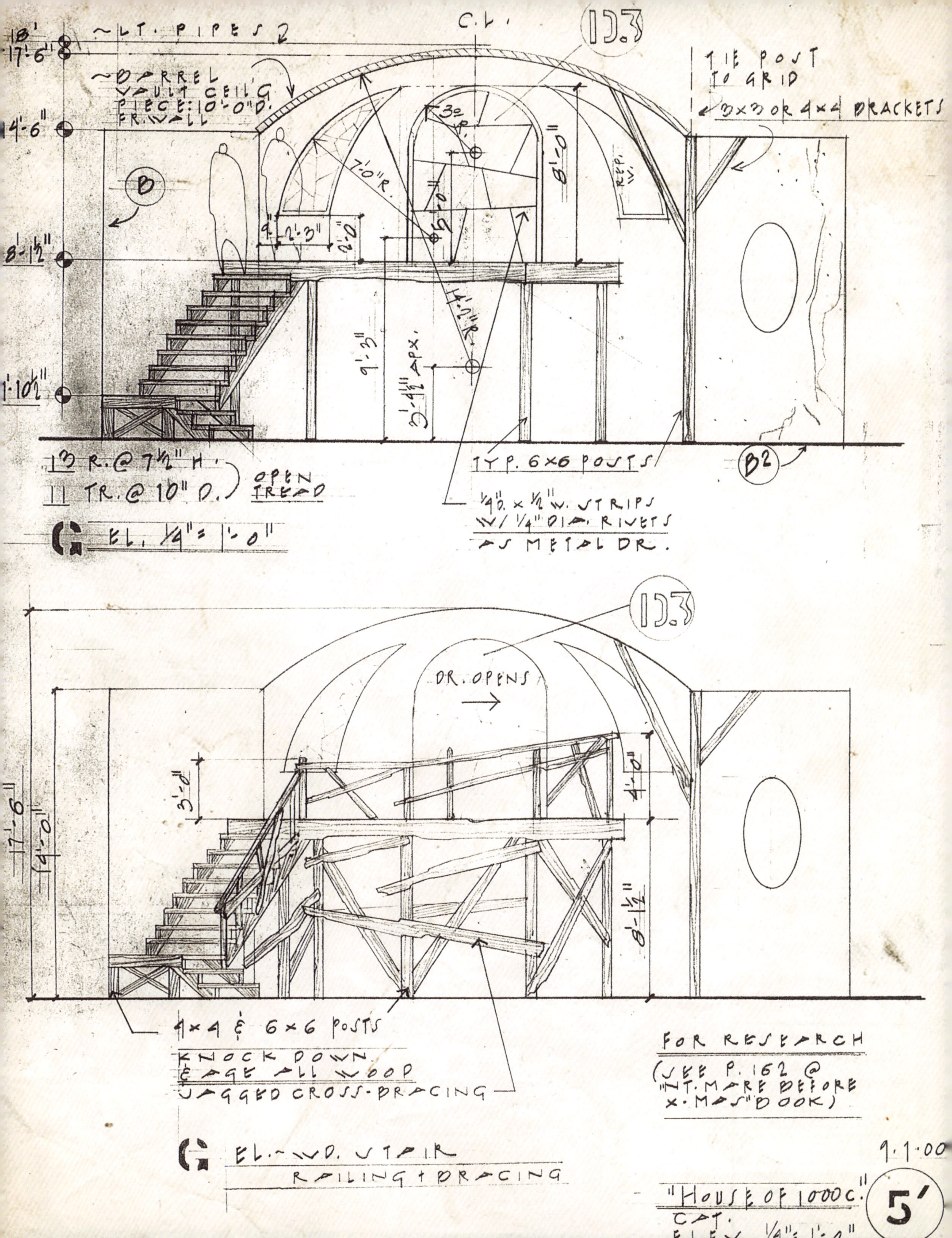

C.L.
LT. PIPES 2
BARREL VAULT CEIL'G PIECE: 10'-0" D. FR. WALL
TIE POST TO GRID
3×3 OR 4×4 BRACKETS
18'
17'-6"
14'-6"
8'-1½"
1'-10½"
7'-0" R.
8'-0"
2'-3"
9'-3"
3'-4½" APX.
TYP. 6×6 POSTS
13 R. @ 7½" H.
11 TR. @ 10" D.
OPEN TREAD
¼" D. × ½" W. STRIPS W/ ¼" DIA. RIVETS AS METAL DR.
G EL. ¼" = 1'-0"
B
B2
DR. OPENS
3'-0"
4'-0"
17'-6"
14'-0"
8'-1½"
4×4 & 6×6 POSTS
KNOCK DOWN
CAGE ALL WOOD
JAGGED CROSS-BRACING
FOR RESEARCH
(SEE P. 162 @ "NT. MARE BEFORE X-MAS" BOOK)
G EL. - WD. STAIR
RAILING + BRACING
9.1.00
"HOUSE OF 1000 C."
CAT.
ELEV. ¼" = 1'-0"
5'

1 INT. PIT -- NIGHT 1

Denise slowly descends the stairs through the dense, thick cobwebbed passageways.

1A INT. PIT -- NIGHT 1A

She reaches the bottom and again is on level ground.

Strange sounds can be heard in the distance.

DENISE
Jerry!

1B INT. PIT -- NIGHT 1B

In the distance a SHADOWY FIGURE stumbles forward. It appears to be Jerry from the shape of the donkey costume...

DENISE
Jerry...
(moving slowly forward)
...is that you?

The figure moves slowly forward.

In the soft light we see it is not Jerry, but a very old heavily bandaged man with a long beard. He is rail thin and covered from head to toe in filthy blood caked wrappings. His eyes are sewn shut.

He is wearing Jerry's donkey head.

DENISE (CONT'D)
Please, help me.

The old man stumbles forward, groaning.

Denise begins to turn and run...THUD! Denis backs straight into another old man. She screams as they grab hold of her clothes and begin to tear at her.

As a piece of her costume comes loose the men recede into the shadows.

Denise is left unharmed wearing the tattered remains of her costume.

2 INT. PIT -- CORPSE ROW -- NIGHT 2

A beaten Denise cautiously searches for Jerry. She moves through heavy iron gates into a long corridor. The walls are lined with the rotted remains of HUMAN BODIES. They are petrified into the rock walls.

(CONTINUED)

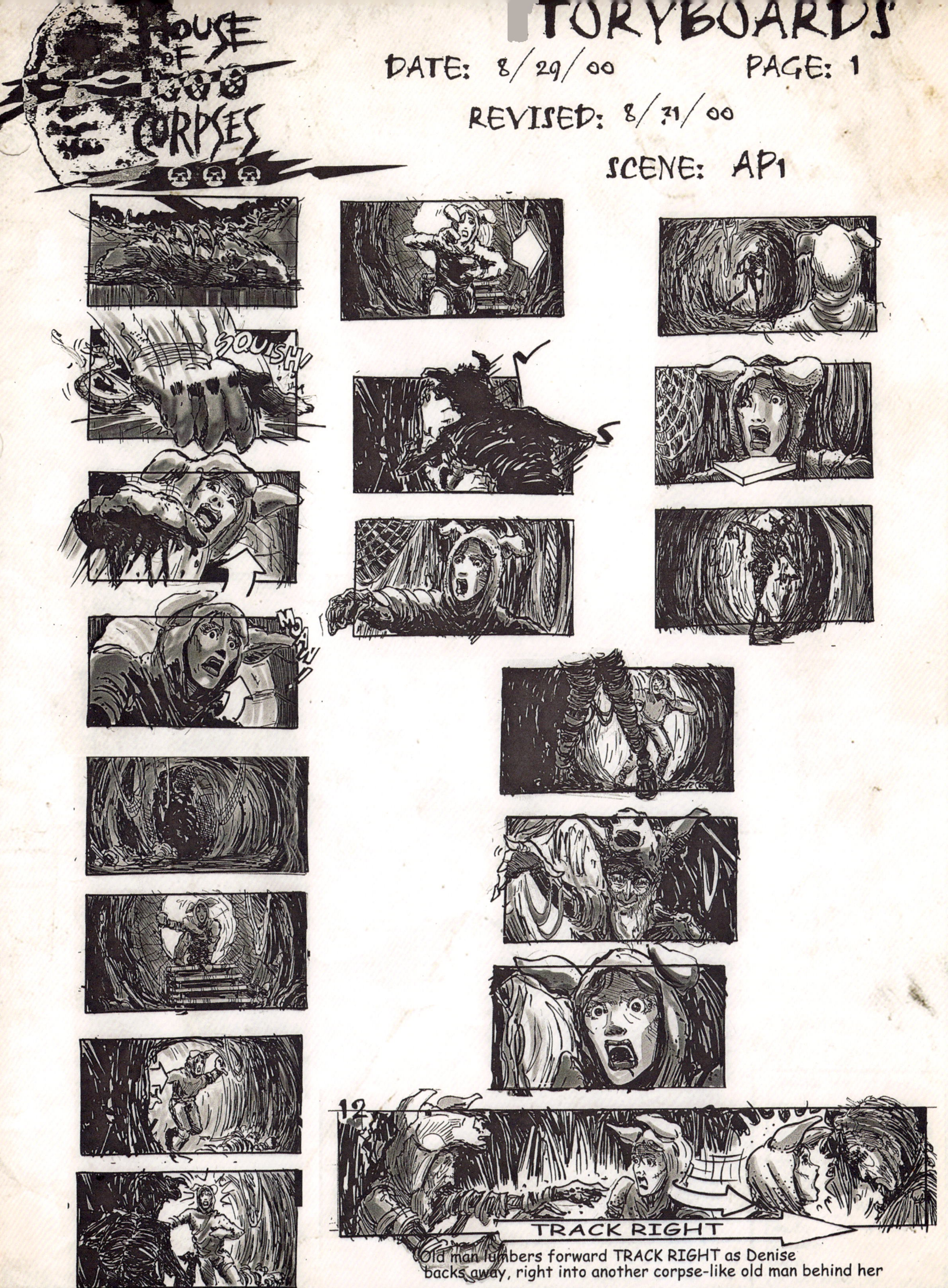
HOUSE OF 1000 CORPSES
STORYBOARDS
DATE: 8/29/00
PAGE: 1
REVISED: 8/31/00
SCENE: AP1
SQUISH!
MOAN!
12
TRACK RIGHT
Old man lumbers forward TRACK RIGHT as Denise
backs away, right into another corpse-like old man behind her

RIP!
RIP!
RIP!
2

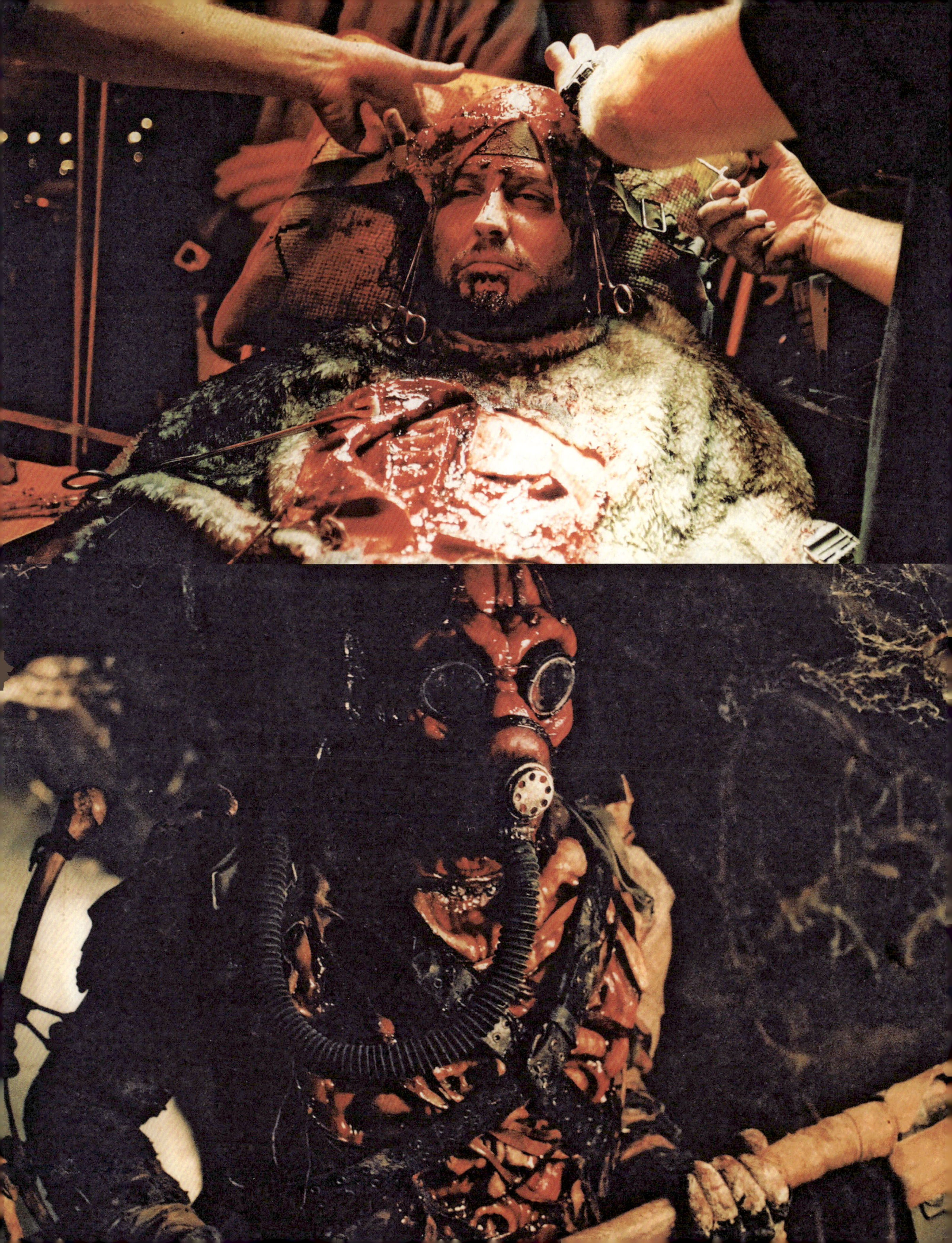

2 CONTINUED: 2

In the distance the moaning is heard, Denise moves towards the sounds.

3 INT. PIT -- CORPSE ROW -- NIGHT 3

Denise cautiously moves down the corridor, the sounds growing louder with each step. The rotted faces stare down at her watching her every move.

The corridor turns sharp and dead ends. Denise stands before a large set of carved wooden doors. She lightly pushes on them. The heavy doors swing open. She steps inside. The doors slam behind her.

4 INT. DEATH CELLS -- NIGHT 4

Denise struggles to open the doors, but finds them locked tight. She proceeds to move deeper into the room. On either side of her are rusted cages.

She peers into one of the darkened cages...Suddenly, a rotted looking man in a harness jumps towards her. He is quickly pulled back like a dog on a chain.

BOOM! Another strange man jumps out from the opposite side. He also is pulled back.

Both men are chained to the walls of their cells.

Denise hears Jerry's cries of pain coming from behind another door.

JERRY
Help me, help me.

DENISE
Jerry are you in here, Jerry where are you?

The chained men mimic Jerry's cries.

Denise pulls open the doors to REVEAL: a SKELETON THIN CORPSE of a man breathing through a clear mask, his arms are supported by steel rods running the length of his body.

Before him stands an operating table, the writhing figure on the table is covered with a sheet. THIS IS DR. SATAN.

Denise stares in shock.

DR. SATAN
(speaking through a box in his throat)
Welcome to Hell...

(CONTINUED)

4a
CREAK
DOOR
DENISE
SLAM!

PEPSI

This section is modified
and looks 100% better
DELTA

4 CONTINUED: 4

Dr. Satan pulls back the sheet to reveal Jerry strapped to the chair, his body has been dissected.

DR. SATAN (CONT'D)
...we've been expecting you.

DENISE
Nooooooooo!

DR. SATAN
Professor!

SLAM! From a balcony above an iron door slides open. Standing in the doorway is THE PROFESSOR: a DEFORMED MUTANT of a man wrapped in a skin and bone suit, he is holding a homemade looking AXE.

Only his face and arms are exposed, they resemble chewed raw meat. He screams a horrible sound from his ragged mouth and charges down from the balcony towards Denise.

Denise turns and runs back through the room of death cells, the inmates howl with evil delight.

The Professor follows, hot on Denise's heels. Denise runs to the only exit, it is locked. The Professor lunges forward swinging his axe, Denise ducks as the Professor smashes his weapon into the doors. The DOORS EXPLODE open.

5 INT. PIT -- CORPSE ROW -- NIGHT 5

Denise stumbles back and continues to run. The Professor pulls his axe from the door and CHARGES after Denise.

6 INT. PIT -- NIGHT 6

Denise runs through the cramped tunnels, having lost sight of the Professor.

She makes a sharp turn and runs head on into The Professor. He swings and misses bringing down a section of the tunnel's ceiling. Denise turns and continues running. The Professor follows.

7 INT. DEADMAN'S CURVE -- PIT -- NIGHT 7

Denise turns a corner and runs into a large dead end. The Professor comes around the corner cutting off her only escape.

He stops and waits, stalking his prey. Denise stands shaking, she looks from side to side...SHE IS TRAPPED.

The Professor, his axe raised to strike, screams and charges towards Denise. Denise ducks and the axe misses her head by inches knocking down a wooden support beam.

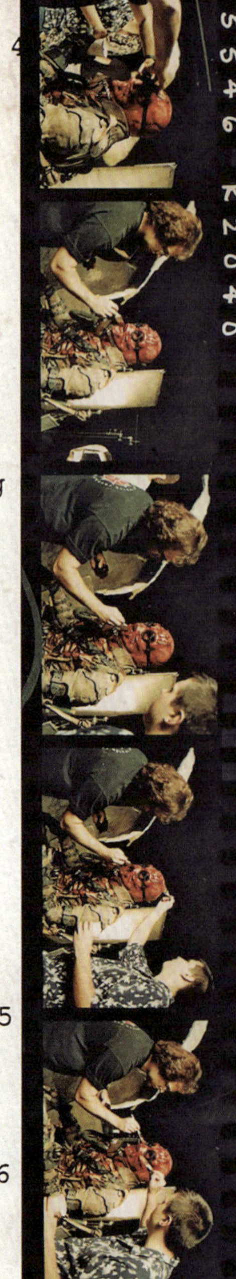

5546 THE HOUSE OF 1000 CORPSES

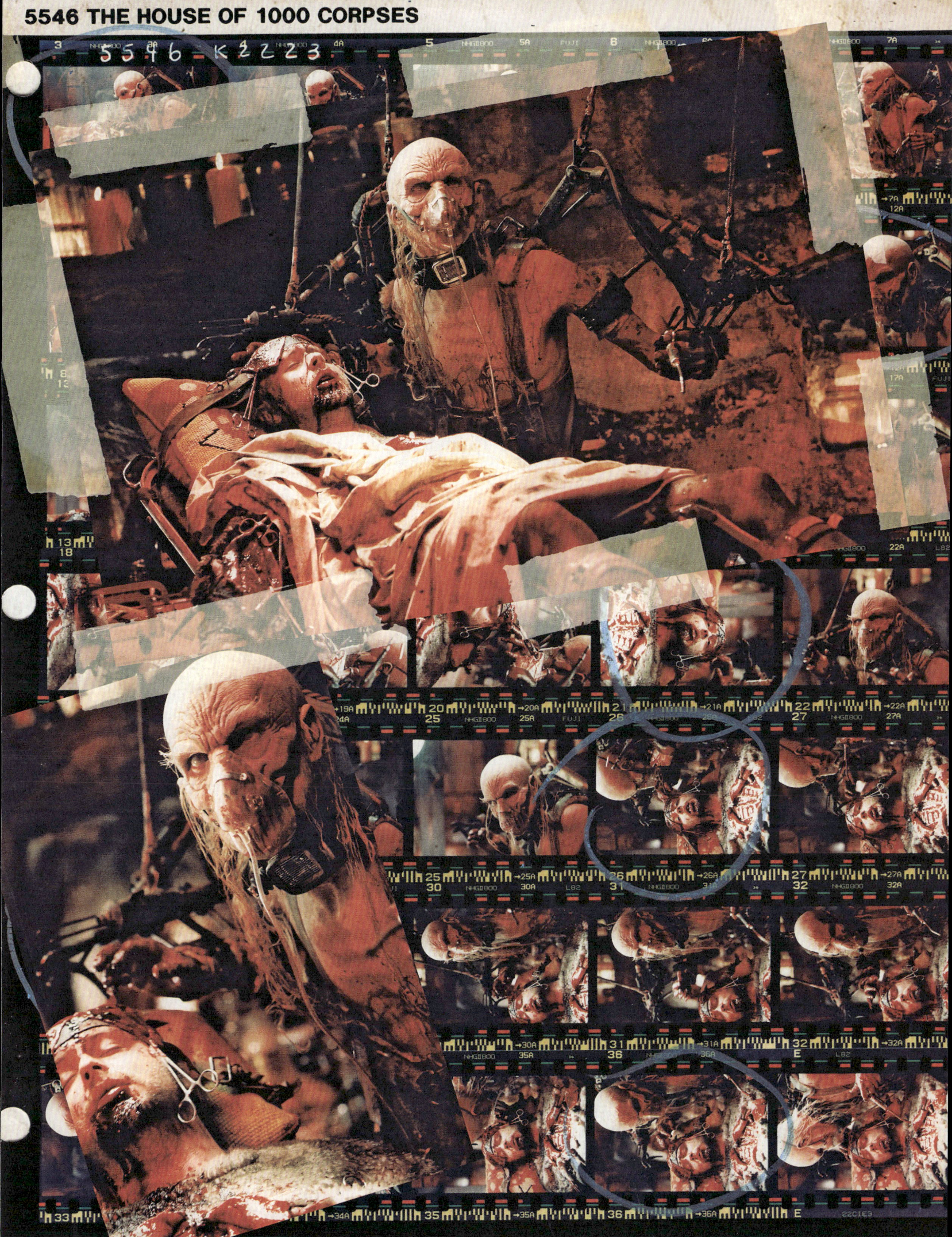

7 CONTINUED: 7

The fallen beam causes the ceiling to come crashing down on Denise and the Professor. They are both completely BURIED ALIVE.

8 EXT. PIT -- MORNING 8

The sun rises up over the trees. Birds are singing, it is a beautiful day.

9 INT. PIT -- DAY 9

Fractured beams of sunlight break through the ground above. Denise, safely buried under a wooden beam, struggles to open her eyes. She pulls herself up through the wreckage and crawls from the pit towards the light above.

The Professor lies motionless, impaled by a wooden beam.

10 EXT. PIT -- DAY 10

Denise climbs up and onto solid ground, she is caked with blood and dirt. She begins to stumble towards the road.

11 EXT. WOODS -- DAY 11

Denise make her way out onto the road. No cars are in sight.

A car comes into view. Denise waves her arms for it to stop. The car comes to a halt.

She runs towards the passenger side door and climbs inside.

12 INT. CAR -- DAY 12

Behind the wheel is Spaulding. Denise is shaking from shock.

DENISE
(weak and soft)
Please...help me.

SPAULDING
Jesus, [girl] what happened to you?

DENISE
I....I.....got away....

SPAULDING
You.. yeah, hey, I recognize you.. I know people been looking for you.

DENISE
(hyperventilating)
I, I, I can't breathe...please take me home.

(CONTINUED)

HG1600 12
→7A
12A
HG1600 13
→8A
CU-1 13A
HG1600 14
→9A
14A
→10A
15
792 15A
→10A
HG1600 16

SLAM!
1
1a
1b
THINGS YOU NEVER SAW BEFORE
OR EVER DREAMED OF!

3
4
5
6
6a
DENISE POV
7
8
..as it collapses hard on top of him
1
1a
2
3
5a
5b

1
2
3
4
7
7A

12 CONTINUED: 12

SPAULDING
Well, don't worry... you are perfectly safe with me.. now just lay back and relax and we'll get you to a doctor.

Silently, Otis sits up in the back seat. He smiles and raises his knife, but says nothing.

MEET THE STARS
OF
THE UPCOMING LION'S GATE FILM
HOUSE OF 1000 CORPSES
SATURDAY
FEBRUARY 1,
2003
2pm
FREE
1000 CORPSES
POSTERS,
STICKERS AND
T-SHIRTS
ROB ZOMBIE
WRITER - DIRECTOR
SID HAIG
"SPAULDING"
SHERI MOON
"BABY"
BILL MOSELEY
"OTIS"
CREATION ENTERTAINMENT'S
COMIC BOOK AND POP CULTURE CONVENTION
PASADENA, CA PASADENA CENTER 300 E. GREEN ST.
for more info go to WWW.CREATIONENT.COM

ILM: House of 1000 Corpses
EVIEW BREAK BOXOFFICE
UTLET: Fangoria
ATE: Nov. 2000
OTES: 1/2
IN THIS

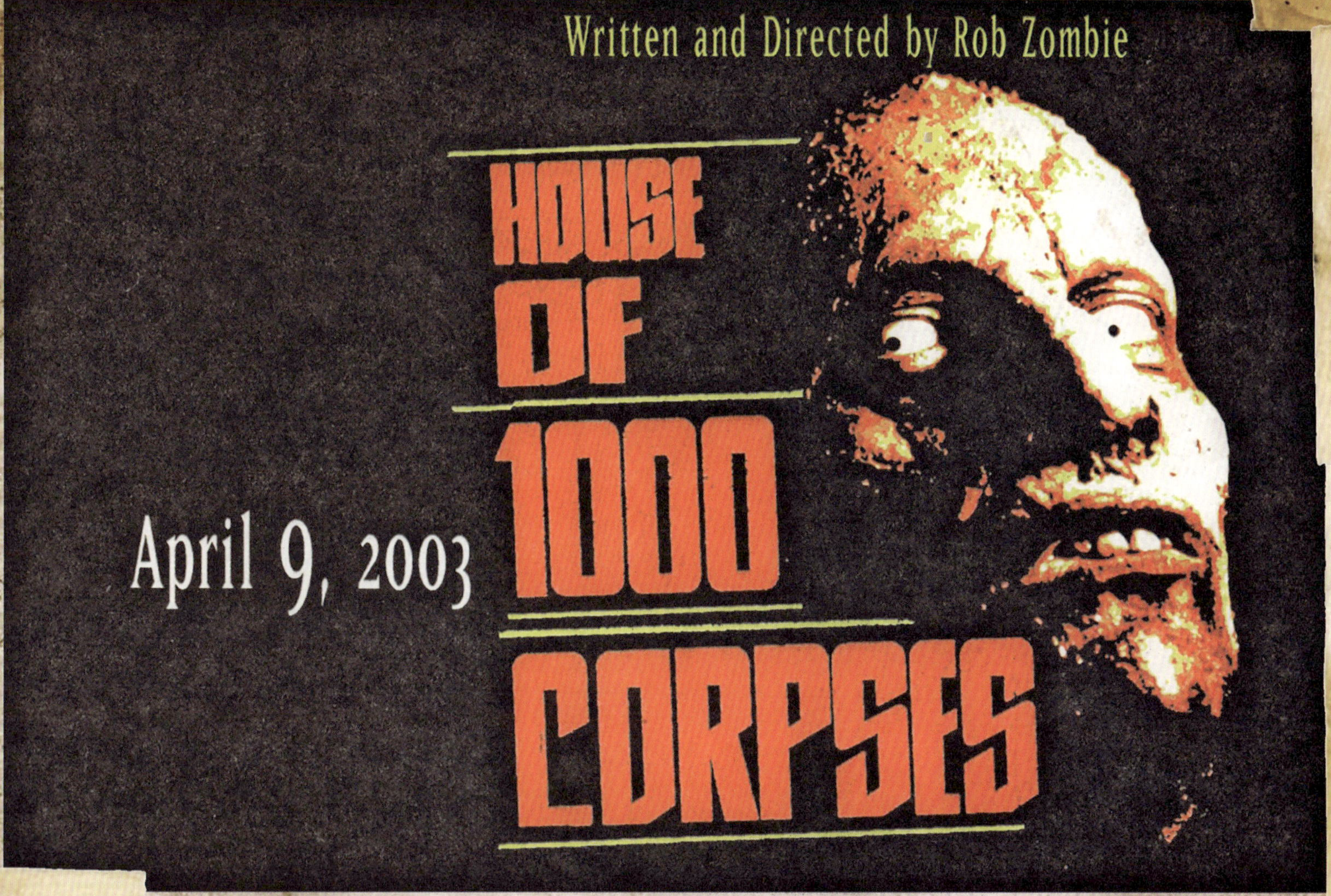

Written and Directed by Rob Zombie

HOUSE OF 1000 CORPSES

April 9, 2003

Cordially invites you and a guest to the premiere of

HOUSE OF 1000 CORPSES

April 9, 2003 7:30 PM SHARP

The ArcLight Cinemas Hollywood 6360 W. Sunset Blvd Hollywood, CA

Party immediately following at Las Palmas 1714 N. Las Palmas

EVENT PRODUCED BY

SUPERMARKET EVENTS

brent bolthouse amanda scheer demme dominique trenier jenifer rosero

Parking located on either Ivar, just below Sunset

(at the side of the complex) or Delongpre (at the back)

Please RSVP to 323.525.2446

This invitation is absolutely non-transferable. Please bring a photo I.D. to the event for check-in.

SEE THE EVIL BRAIN SURGEON KNOWN AS DOCTOR SATAN

COVER ART – GRAHAM HUMPHREYS
COLOR ILLUSTRATIONS – DAVID HARTMAN
CHARACTER SKETCHES – ROB ZOMBIE

PHOTOS, SKETCHES AND SET DESIGNS COURTESY OF GREGG GIBBS

MAKEUP DEPARTMENT PHOTOS COURTESY OF WAYNE TOTH

SPECIAL THANKS TO THE CAST AND CREW. WITHOUT YOU ALL THERE WOULDN'T BE A MOVIE

FUN 4 THE WHOLE FAMILY

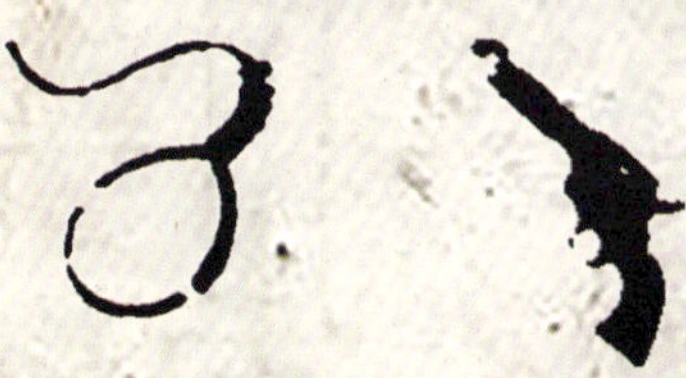

EXPERIENCE REAL LIFE HORROR

HOUSE OF
1000 CORPSES

PO Box 3088
San Rafael, CA 94912
www.insighteditions.com

Find us on Facebook: www.facebook.com/InsightEditions
Follow us on Instagram: @insighteditions

Publisher's note: The script pages in this book have been reprinted in their original form to preserve authenticity and have not been edited for grammar, spelling, or word choice.

Trade Edition: ISBN: 979-8-3374-0202-4
Portfolio Edition ISBN: 979-8-3374-0294-9

Publisher: Raoul Goff
SVP, Group Publisher: Vanessa Lopez
VP, Creative: Chrissy Kwasnik
VP, Manufacturing: Alix Nicholaeff
Art Director: Matt Girard
Senior Editor: Adrienne Procaccini
Editorial Assistant: Audrey Salo
Executive Managing Editor: Maria Spano
Senior Production Manager: Greg Steffen
Strategic Production Planner: Lina s Palma-Temena

Interior design by Rob Zombie

REPLANTED PAPER

Insight Editions, in association with Roots of Peace, will plant two trees for each tree used in the manufacturing of this book. Roots of Peace is an internationally renowned humanitarian organization dedicated to eradicating land mines worldwide and converting war-torn lands into productive farms and wildlife habitats. Roots of Peace will plant two million fruit and nut trees in Afghanistan and provide farmers there with the skills and support necessary for sustainable land use.

Manufactured in China

10 9 8 7 6 5 4 3 2 1

WRITTEN &
BY